LYTTON STRA

Michael Holroyd's first edition of *Lytton Strachey* was published in 1967–8, followed six years later by *Augustus John* and in 1988–92 by *Bernard Shaw*, confirming him as one of the great modern biographers. *Lytton Strachey: The New Biography* is published by Chatto & Windus.

LYTTON STRACHEY BY HIMSELF

A Self-Portrait

Edited and introduced by
Michael Holroyd

VINTAGE

A VINTAGE BOOK

Published by Vintage 1994

2 4 6 8 10 9 7 5 3 1

Copyright © Alix Strachey and Michael Holroyd 1971

First published in Great Britain by William Heinemann Ltd 1971

Vintage
Random House, 20 Vauxhall Bridge Road, London SW1V 2SA

Random House Australia (Pty) Limited
20 Alfred Street, Milsons Point, Sydney
New South Wales, 2061, Australia

Random House New Zealand Limited
18 Poland Road, Glenfield,
Auckland 10, New Zealand

Random House South Africa (Pty) Limited
PO Box 337, Bergvlei, South Africa

Random House UK Limited Reg. No. 954009

A CIP catalogue record for this book
is available from the British Library

ISBN 0 09 938741 7

Set in 10½/12 Sabon by
Deltatype Ltd, Ellesmere Port, Cheshire

Printed and bound in Great Britain by
Cox & Wyman, Reading, Berkshire

CONTENTS

CONTENTS

INTRODUCTION

'I NEVER TRAVEL without my diary,' says Gwendolen in *The Importance of Being Earnest*. 'One should always have something sensational to read in the train.'

Intermittently throughout his life Lytton Strachey kept a diary, but by today's standards none of them are sensational. They were written, on the whole, in a lower key than his letters. 'No good letter', he tells us in an essay on Horace Walpole, 'was ever written to convey information or to please the recipient: it may achieve both these results incidentally; but its fundamental purpose is to express the personality of the writer.' Strachey himself was a copious letter-writer, and his correspondence conveys many aspects of his personality very vividly. But his letters *were* written, at least in part, to please their recipients. The Strachey we see in these letters is among friends; his diaries reveal him by himself.

The first two diaries he kept, at the ages of ten and eleven, were obedient documents, composed almost in automatic response to the literary atmosphere in which he grew up. Spurred on by Lady Strachey, he and his brothers and sisters were perpetually producing magazines, turning out quantities of verse, filling notebooks with playlets, grappling with literary puzzles, and copying down passages from Shakespeare. Lytton's own contributions, to judge from these first short diaries, were nothing exceptional. They are amusing, as many children's pieces are, for their combination of directness and inconsequence. What was unusual for a boy of this age was the absence of boasting, the honesty and odd self-deflationary humour: 'I had some shots at buoys passing with a smaller gun and hit once and missed five times!'

But perhaps the most interesting aspect of these pieces is their revelation of the literary pressure surrounding all the Strachey children. 'Mamma read the Iliad' sounds like some chorus almost sinister in its repetition.

The journal Strachey kept of his travels between December 1892 and May 1893 was also started as something of a duty. It was not really a private diary at all: it was almost certain to be read by his family once he got home. Yet there is no sense of constriction or self-consciousness in the writing, little feeling of anyone reading over his shoulder.

The voyages he describes acted as a temporary release from the dark womb of Lancaster Gate, that architectural mon-strosity which so shadowed his spirit. The atmosphere of these adventures is one of blue sea-skies and blue hills in the distance, the 'heavenly music' of military bands, and 'wondrous sights' – mirages and octopuses and powdered horses – which so intoxicated him that 'Oh! it is like some beautiful dream'. From this enchantment he awoke only after he was back in Lancaster Gate, and, like Caliban, cried to dream again.

Perhaps because he had escaped some distance from the confining circle of his family, he is able to reveal his personality in these pages with great clarity. He seems to have been a curious mixture of precociousness and conservatism. His precociousness was partly the result of a rapidly developing mind with its capacity for clear expression, partly a sensitivity to other people which told him what to say, and when to say nothing. He had a natural gift for treating, without incivility, all grown-ups as his equals, and this spared him the embarrass-ment of adults behaving towards him like children. Quite self-sufficient in his manner, he gave little trouble and was seen by many as being extraordinarily mature. But this 'maturity' was really a camouflage, a means of concealing his natural shyness. He did not break up his social timidity or his obsessive self-awareness; he skated successfully round them. So they remained intact to block later on the direct expression of his emotions. Passion, tragedy, outrage, boredom – such things he would convey by humour, often a deflective irony which was his 'criticism of life'.

In one sense, Strachey was 'older' at this time than at any other stage of his career. His conservatism was pretty well absolute. It was a romantic quality, and largely visual. He was alive to all the nice distinctions of what rank might inspect the guard on what occasions, of differences in uniform and the rivalries of regiments. He even rose from his bed at 6am to catch sight of some soldiers disembarking at Cape Town. 'The Cape Highlanders (volunteers) played the pipes as they were marching away. They did look so lovely especially after their sea kit which consists of blue trousers and coats and Neapolitan fishermen's hats, only blue. As they marched off there seemed a great many of them, although there was only half a regiment. The Cape Highlanders think themselves far superior to the Black Watch!!!' A few months later, he became highly indignant on learning that his uncle was resigning his commission and returning to the drabness of civilian life. 'I am most disgusted with Uncle Charlie for leaving the army,' he told his mother.

Like many semi-invalids, Strachey loved travelling, and his life-long appetite for travel was almost certainly whetted by this first journey. It was, as he explains, 'a unique experience', and the pages in which he describes it form a unique journal. The mood throughout is light and delicious. He does not weigh it down, as so many boys of twelve or thirteen would have been tempted to do, with chunks of 'important' geographical and historical information. His descriptions are brief and vivid, as he conveys his personal response to all he can see, 'with the aid of spectacles', around him. The world was a mysterious but uncomplicated place, full of magical beauty and thrilling adventures – donkey rides, pyramids and marvellous carnivals. Above all he communicates his brimming sense of enjoyment. It is an infectiously happy diary.

It also displays distinct literary ability, especially a natural talent for narrative. Strachey was a keenly observant boy, already slightly cynical about such human frailties as vanity and pride:

> At the end of the table was a young man called d'Alton he went in for being funny, he is very short and small, dark, with a *very* curly moustachio which he twirled with pride . . .
>
> There was an old man close by fishing with a bamboo. After some time he caught a beautiful fish about one foot six long, then killed it and put [it] in a nitch in the rock . . . He was so pleased with his success that he began smoking a cigar.

His tone is one of controlled astonishment which sometimes lifts the story very agreeably to the edge of farce:

> Aunt Aggie said she thought it would be a good idea to go to the sphinx on camels, directly she mentioned this word fifteen camels were on us, all making the most awful noise when sitting down. We were all seized by at least four men who pulled us in four different directions I got to a camel and an Arab said it was a lady's one, which it was not so I was hussled off and two men came and lifted me into the air and put [me] on a camel at this moment the sheik interfered and I got onto the one that was supposed to have had a lady's saddle. It was rather a ghastly sensation when the camel got up and you thought you were going to tumble off. We walked on our camels to the sphinx where we dismounted and walked to a place just opposite its face. Although its nose had entirely gone it looked as if all its features were there. What an exquisite face it is – how solemn –how majestic you look, your eyes looking out into the desert with that beautiful expression always on your face so colossal and so perfect. You, who have been there for thousands and thousands of years, you, who have gazed and gazed at that endless sea of sand ever since you existed, tell me oh tell me how to look with that sublime expression on your face at all that comes and all that goes, careless of everything for ever.

Such a passage contains many of the Stracheyesque ingredients that were to make up his mature style: the wonderfully comic focus; the dramatic narrative gift; the romantic and rhetorical rhapsodizing which, slightly overpitched, sometimes overshoots the effect for which it strives.

The mood of all his later diaries is different. Those that were the 'outcome of excitements' – for example, those of August 1905 and of May 1919 – are never sustained. The process of

writing was always a lonely and inhospitable business for him.
It was much more intriguing to whisper his secrets to people
rather than commit them coldly to paper. For Strachey was to
find his natural balance by becoming involved, simul-
taneously, with two types of people: the lover and the
confidant. He fell deeply in love about half a dozen times
during his life, and parallel to this band of inamoratos there
stretched a line of brother and sister confessors to whom he
poured out the narrative of his passion. The first of these
intimate friends was Leonard Woolf; and he was succeeded by
Maynard Keynes, James Strachey, Ottoline Morrell, Carrington and Mary Hutchinson. These people took the place of his
diaries, which would have disappeared altogether had his
amatory arrangements worked out more tidily. As it was,
lovers and confidants sometimes became entangled or else
involved with other parties who were already inter-dependent,
forming a complex cat's cradle of relationships. Then there
were other times when everything would dissolve and Strachey
was alone. It was during these solitary periods that his diaries
reappear.

Not until he got to Cambridge did Strachey find anyone
whom he could trust as his confessor. Before that, at Leamington and Liverpool, he had relied on diaries alone. At
Leamington, for instance, when he became infatuated with
another boy, he put down his thoughts and feelings about it in
a secret book. This book, giving us a glimpse into his life at a
crucially formative stage, is of great biographical interest. But
from Strachey's own point of view, a diary was not an ideal
method of describing such episodes. It could be lost, could run
the risk of being read by unsympathetic strangers. The thought
of such dangers was inhibiting. For both these diaries revealed
his homosexuality. The first was written while Oscar Wilde
was in Reading Gaol, the second soon after Wilde went into
humiliating exile in France.

The Liverpool diary is a cry for love. 'The truth is, I want
companionship,' he writes. He had no real friends, and was
desperately lonely. At times his isolation seems almost to have
obliterated his personality, extinguishing his sense of existence

—but the diary flourished. He began it, he tells us, 'in the veriest dog days imaginable', for a special purpose. 'I hope it will fulfil the office of safety-valve to my morbidity, which otherwise will become too much to put up with and will have to be abolished.' But there are some amusing sketches of academics and of middle-class society in Liverpool, and a realistic description of the slums which seemed to mirror back at him his physical self-disgust:

> Nearly every street is a slum in this town, except those with fine shops. Here is nothing intermediate. Hardly anyone lives in the town if they can possibly help it. Pitt Street was painful to me in the extreme; it stank; dirty 'furriners' wandered in groups over it; and a dingy barrel organ rattled its jargon in the yard . . . I met an old man today, haggard, and pitiful to behold. His cheeks were a hectic red, and his eyes looked out on me with the weary, desolate expression of one lost and drifting. He tottered along the road in an access of decrepitude, his ragged overcoat clutched over his frail form . . .
>
> . . . In the afternoon walked down to the docks and thence to the landing stage. The crowds of people were appalling. The landing stage blocked; and *all* hideous. It gave me the shivers in two minutes and I fled. My self-conscious vanity is really most painful. As I walk through the streets I am agonized by the thoughts of my appearance. Of course it is hideous, but what *does* it matter? I only make it worse by peering into people's faces to see what they are thinking. And the worst of it is I hate myself for doing it.

Solitude, failure, the 'absolument rien' of Liverpool life, and especially the conviction of his own outcast ugliness – these are the dominant themes of this diary. 'When I consider that I am now eighteen years of age a shudder passes through my mind and I hardly dare look at the creature those years have made me.' This is a far cry from the gingerbread figure of Bloomsbury legend, the 'extravagant old stage duchess whinnying and trumpeting her pronouncements over the teacups', as P. N. Furbank pictured him. It is also very far from the Strachey who was shortly to establish himself, by personality and wit, as a pre-eminent figure at Cambridge. Here he reveals the darker side of himself. 'I wonder if I shall ever fall "in love". I can't help smiling at the question – if they only knew – if they only knew! But it is a tragedy also.' This is the other face of that comedy which made up so much of his high-stepping life, a face unseen even by some of his friends who consequently did not take his love-affairs seriously. Love was an escape from the sort of intense loneliness he delineates here, his method of relinquishing all that he hated in himself. It was important.

Strachey's Liverpool diary appears to have been successful for a time in redressing the balance between the glamour of his fantasies and the degrading spectacle he felt he made of himself in public. But in the end it seems to have increased his self-preoccupation, and he abandoned it.

The last journal of his life, 'A Fortnight in France', was also written in solitude – but this was a solitude of his choosing. By now he was able to contemplate his own image with stylized equanimity:

> Looking at myself in a shop-window mirror I saw for the first time how completely grey my hair was over my temples. So that had come at last! I was beginning to think it never would. Do I feel like it? Perhaps I do a little – a very little. A certain sense of detachment declares itself amid the agitations that continue to strew my path.

This journal is by far his most polished performance as a diarist, and shows what he might have achieved in that vein had his life turned out differently. It is a marvellously fluent piece, full of humour and tenderness, remembrances of loves past and speculations over the future, all effortlessly inter-woven. Perhaps better than anything else he wrote, 'A Fortnight in France' conveys the peculiar charm that entranced so many men and women who knew him, and that is often elusive on paper. His stream of consciousness, intensified by solitude, is not entirely uninhibited; there is something slightly contrived: but that was the man. There is little sign too of the stomach cancer that, within five months, would kill him – just some fatigue and a lengthening detachment from life (he is very much the spectator). The vacuous boredom of his early days is long since past – he had experienced almost too much. Like Hazlitt, he had 'had a happy life', and there is much sheer entertainment in these pages, mixed with some wistfulness. Describing the wine cellars of Reims, he wrote:

> In the middle of the endless avenues, about half a dozen slaves – sweet creatures – sat bottling and corking the wine. Impossible to speak to them, as the odious cripple who was showing me round gave no possible opportunity for any such thing. All I could do, as I vanish down one of the avenues, was to wave my hand to them – and I'm glad to say they waved back.

At the beginning of the Liverpool diary Strachey warns us that 'there will be little recorded here that is not transitory, and there will be much here that is quite untrue. The inquisitive reader should he peep between the covers will find anything but myself – who perhaps after all do not exist but in my own phantasy.' This, of course, was a defensive gambit; all these diaries point light into strange corners of his character. But what is true is that they do not portray the whole man.

To remedy this I have incorporated in this volume some other autobiographical writings – pieces such as the facetious 'First and Last Will and Testament' and his address to the Conscientious Objectors Tribunal – that show him in a more public role. The most important of these writings are his two long autobiographical essays 'Lancaster Gate' and 'Monday June 26th 1916', both of which he read to the Memoir Club.

The Memoir Club was founded in March 1920. Besides Strachey, it consisted of twelve members: Clive and Vanessa Bell, E. M. Forster, Roger Fry, Duncan Grant, Maynard Keynes, Desmond and Molly MacCarthy, Adrian Stephen, Saxon Sydney-Turner and Leonard and Virginia Woolf. The club had developed out of an earlier play-reading and Novel Club invented to bring Desmond MacCarthy to the point of writing his novel, which had collapsed once it was discovered that MacCarthy was speaking spontaneously from blank sheets of paper. It was joined later by some members of the Caroline Club, founded by David Garnett and Francis Birrell as a rival to the Novel Club.

Over a period of thirty-six years the Memoir Club would meet, two or three times a year, dine at a restaurant, and then listen to one or two of its members reading aloud some reminiscences. Several of the group had been Cambridge 'Apostles', so it comes as no surprise to learn that 'absolute frankness' was insisted upon. One of the long-term achievements of the club was the part it later played in bringing into existence books such as David Garnett's and Leonard Woolf's autobiographies, Virginia Woolf's biography of Roger Fry, and possibly even Desmond MacCarthy's *Humanities* (1953). The two brilliant papers Keynes delivered have been published in book form as *Two Memoirs* (1949).

Strachey read 'Lancaster Gate' to the Memoir Club in 1922. *Queen Victoria* had been published the year before, and he was now at the height of his fame and literary powers. With the single exception of *Elizabeth and Essex*, all his books were based on the essay form. Although he longed to write drama and lyric poetry, it was the essay that suited his style and stamina best, and 'Lancaster Gate' must be accounted one of his finest essays. Its remarkable evocation of atmosphere, its passages of glorious comedy, its analysis of the physiological effects produced on him by that pink-and-black pile in which he grew up have been orchestrated by a masterly hand. Here is the clue to Strachey's attitude towards the Victorians; here is the clue to so much in his life. 'To reconstruct, however dimly, that grim machine, would be to realize with some real distinctness the essential substance of my biography,' he writes. And in reconstructing it, he unconsciously shows it as a womb in which his nature was entangled, and out of which he had to be born again in order to achieve any sort of freedom and fulfilment.

Strachey remained acutely susceptible to architecture all his life, from the 'lovely musharabiyeh windows and sweet arches' of an Egyptian mosque to Blenheim Palace, which, he told Mary Hutchinson, is 'entrancing, and life-enhancing. I wish it were mine. It is enormous, but one would not feel it too big. The grounds are beautiful too, and there is a bridge over a lake which positively gives one an erection.' Every building he subconsciously compared with Lancaster Gate. But his description of the place is not objective – an estate agent would be prosecuted for it. He magnified its size because of its extraordinary effect upon him; and he exaggerated certain features of his home life because he was an hysteric given, in all his writing, to dramatic extremes. It is possible, too, that his obstinate illnesses, which developed only after his younger brother James was born (when Lytton was already in his eighth year) were a means of attracting attention to himself. Similarly, it seems likely that his hysteria formation had its origins in the influence of the Lancaster Gate régime upon him. Yet his exaggerations are not untruthful. 'The life that began then – my Lancaster Gate life – was to continue till I was twenty-eight,' he writes, '—a man full grown – all the changes from childhood to adolescence, from youth to manhood, all the developments, the curiosities, the pains, the passions, the despairs, the delights, of a quarter of a century having taken place within those walls.' No one could guess from reading this sentence the large amount of time he had spent away from his home – his boarding schools, his holidays in Rothiemurchus, his frequent travels in France and Italy, his two years in Liverpool, six years at Cambridge. Yet the presence of Lancaster Gate did pervade these years, and however long he might stay away, however far he might go, he could not get beyond its magnetic pull.

The second paper he read to the Memoir Club, 'Monday June 26th 1916', was not written specifically for this group, which had not yet been formed. Like 'Lancaster Gate', it is an autobiographical fragment of lasting value, yet it is wholly dissimilar. For here Strachey breaks new ground as a writer. Abandoning his usual Procrustean technique, he gives a minute reconstruction of a day on which nothing in particular happens, a day spent with friends in talk and strolls and tea and ingenious stratagems concocted for the pursuit of love and in the cause of personal relationships. Instead of ironic compression and prefabricated shape – what Max Beerbohm called 'the serpent swallowing its own tail' – he uses a linear, even a tangential method of composition, similar in some ways to that of Virginia Woolf. Everything is set down with trance-like exactitude and with an unsparing analysis of motives, especially his own; yet as an evocation of Bloomsbury it will probably convert no one. Those who detest the group will be confirmed in their antipathy by this picture of a life of crowded leisure and of easy privilege in the midst of war. Others will be fascinated by what is a unique view of this gifted circle, a spontaneous and brilliant piece of writing, without parallel in Lytton Strachey's career.

Except for 'Lancaster Gate', which is the only retrospective piece in the book, I have placed everything in chronological order, and supplied linking passages to make it easier to read each instalment in its proper context. Other editorial inter-ferences I have tried to keep to a minimum. The result, I hope, is an intermittent but not disconnected miniature auto-biography of the man whom the critic Gabriel Merle has called 'the sphinx of Bloomsbury'.

MICHAEL HOLROYD

GILES LYTTON STRACHEY *was born at Stowey House, Clapham Common, on 1 March 1880, the eleventh of thirteen children, three of whom died in infancy.*

His father, General (Sir) Richard Strachey, then in his sixty-third year, had passed most of his active career in India. A man of prodigious versatility, he had been not only a soldier but a meteorologist, botanist, fine geographical scholar, explorer, engineer, mathematician, civil administrator and, in his spare time, a competent water-colour painter. He extended the Indian railways and canals, established the first adequate forest service, reorganized the Public Works Department and instigated financial and administrative measures that were pronounced by the jurist Sir Henry Maine to be the greatest reforms carried out in that country during his time there. Few men had done so much, often in ways unknown to the outside world, for the development of modern India.

While out there he had gained the reputation for being a forceful character with a somewhat peppery temper. But back in England he grew milder, rather vague, and detached from much that was going on around him. Lytton's earliest memories of him recalled little but the sheaves of paper, the voluminous sheets covered with elaborate calculations, that, to the last, encumbered his desk. In the evenings he was seldom seen without a novel in his hand, reading steadily and indiscriminately through six novels a week. During the day he would work in his study at railway and atmospheric matters, perfecting his instruments for measuring the movements of clouds.

The dominating figure during Lytton's childhood and adolescence was undoubtedly his mother. The daughter of Sir John Peter Grant and Henrietta Chichele, she had met Richard Strachey in India, and married him on 4 January 1859. At the time of Lytton's birth she was only thirty-nine, and it was partly due to this wide difference in age between father and mother that her presence was so much more keenly felt in the home, especially by the younger children. She was a woman of tremendous vigour and haphazard ways: no intellectual, but extremely well-read, especially in French literature and Elizabethan drama; a strong supporter of the Women's Progressive Movement who was admired by many eminent men and women of the day including George Eliot, Lord Lytton and Fitzjames Stephen; and an addict to parlour games, puzzles and billiards which she played constantly. She had no taste in the plastic arts, but was a great lover of music.

In appearance Lady Strachey was a majestic figure, invariably dressed in long sweeping clothes of black satin. Yet her movements were ungainly, and her statuesque looks were not enhanced by successive attacks of vertigo — one of which led to her arrest near Marble Arch on suspicion of drunkenness. Her moods, too, were unpredictable. A passionate conversationalist, her arguments were impeded by bouts of absentmindedness, during which she would wander off to some far distant room, gaze around it in distraction for several minutes trying to recall why she was there, then return to the original conversation and argue her point of view with extreme urgency, as if making up for lost time.

The Stracheys moved into 69 Lancaster Gate in 1884 and remained there until the summer of 1907 when, depleted in numbers, they moved to a smaller house in Hampstead. Leonard Woolf, who visited Lancaster Gate at the turn of the century, has given a description of the Strachey régime there that complements the picture in Lytton Strachey's essay.

At dinner someone might casually say something which implied that he remembered George IV (which he might) or even Voltaire or Warren Hastings, and certainly to Lytton the eighteenth century was more congenial and, in a sense, more

*real than the nineteenth or the twentieth. The atmosphere of
the dining-room at Lancaster Gate was that of British history
and of that comparatively small ruling middle class which for
the last 100 years had been the principal makers of British
history.*

> *At supper on Sunday evenings in Lancaster Gate . . . the
> number of Strachey's present was to a visitor at first bewilder-
> ing . . . The level of intelligence in each son and daughter and in
> the father and mother was incredibly, fantastically high. They
> were all, like their mother, passionately intellectual, most of
> them with very quick minds and lively imaginations. All of
> them, I suspect, except the two eldest, must have been born
> with pens in their hands and perhaps spectacles on their noses.
> Their chief recreation was conversation and they adored
> conversational speculation which usually led to argument . . .
> When six or seven Stracheys became involved in an argument
> over the dinner table, as almost always happened, the roar and
> rumble, the shrill shrieks, the bursts of laughter, the sound and
> fury of excitement were deafening and to an unprepared
> stranger paralysing.*[1]

*Though the shell of 69 Lancaster Gate remains the same
today, the interior has been merged with the houses on either
side and is unrecognizable. In May 1959 the Stracheys' old
home became part of Douglas House, the large American
Forces Club which occupied Nos. 66–71 Lancaster Gate. It is
now (1994) part of the Charles Dickens Hotel.*

[1] *Sowing* by Leonard Woolf (1961) pp. 190–1

LANCASTER GATE

THE INFLUENCE OF houses on their inhabitants might well be the subject of a scientific investigation. Those curious contraptions of stones or bricks, with all their peculiar adjuncts, trimmings, and furniture, their specific immutable shapes, their intense and inspissated atmosphere, in which our lives are entangled as completely as our souls in our bodies – what powers do they not wield over us, what subtle and pervasive effects upon the whole substance of our existence may not be theirs? Or is that all nonsense? Our fathers, no doubt, would have laughed at such a speculation; for to our fathers the visible conformations of things were unimportant; they were more interested in the mental and moral implication of their surroundings than in the actual nature of them; and their spirits, so noble and oblivious, escaped the direct pressure of the material universe. They could understand that it would make a difference whether one spent one's life in an ancient family seat in Gloucestershire or in a red-brick villa in Tooting – the social, personal, and traditional distinctions were obvious enough. But the notion that the proportions of a bedroom, for instance, might be significant would have appeared absurd to them; and so they were able to create, and to inhabit, South Kensington almost unconsciously, as if such conduct were the most natural thing in the world. Our view is different. We find satisfaction in curves and colours, and windows fascinate us, we are agitated by staircases, inspired by doors, disgusted by cornices, depressed by chairs, made wanton by ceilings, entranced by passages, and exacerbated by a rug.

In my case at any rate the impression caused by a house has been profound and extraordinary. I say impression, because as to more remote effects – such is the subtlety and complexity of the question – I hardly know what they may have been, or even whether there were any; but a memorable impression is beyond a doubt. Of all my dreams (and I am a confirmed dreamer) there is one alone which persistently recurs, only slightly varying in its details, with a curious iteration. For some reason or another – one of those preposterous and yet absolutely satisfying reasons which occur in dreams – we are back again, once more, just as we were, in Lancaster Gate. We are in the drawing-room, among the old furniture, arranged in the old way, and it is understood that we are to go there indefinitely, as if we had never left it. The strange thing is that, when I realize that this has come about, that our successive wanderings have been a mere interlude, that we are once more permanently established at number 69, a feeling of intimate satisfaction comes over me. I am positively delighted. And this is strange because, in my working life, I have never for a moment, so far as I am aware, regretted our departure from that house, and if, in actuality, we *were* to return to it, I can imagine nothing which would disgust me more. So, when I wake up, and find myself after all at Gordon Square or Tidmarsh, I have the odd sensation of a tremendous relief at finding that my happiness of one second before was a delusion.

Apart from my pleasure at it, no doubt it is hardly surprising that Lancaster Gate should haunt me. For it was a portentous place, and I spent in it the first twenty-five years of my conscious life. My remembrances of Stowey House are dim and sporadic – Jim Rendel[1] with a penny in a passage – a miraculous bean at the bottom of the garden – Beatrice Chamberlain[2] playing at having tea with me, with leaves and

[1] James Meadows Rendel, Chairman of the Assam Bengal Railway and an expert on Poor Law administration, who had married Lytton's eldest sister, Elinor.
[2] The eldest daughter of Joseph Chamberlain and his first wife Harriet Kenrick, she was a half-sister to Neville Chamberlain.

acorns, under a tree. But my consecutive existence began in the nursery at Lancaster Gate – the nursery that I can see now, empty and odd and infinitely elevated, as it was when I stood in it for the first time at the age of four with my mother, and looked out of the window at the surprisingly tall houses opposite, and was told that this was where we were going to live. A calm announcement – received with some excitement, which was partly caused by the unusual sensation of extreme height, as I peered at the street below. The life that began then – my Lancaster Gate life – was to continue till I was twenty-eight – a man full grown – all the changes from childhood to adolescence, from youth to manhood, all the developments, the curiosities, the pains, the passions, the despairs, the delights, of a quarter of a century having taken place within those walls.

A portentous place! Yes, but exactly how portentous it is not easy to convey. Its physical size was no doubt the most obviously remarkable thing about it; but it was not mere size, it was size gone wrong, size pathological; it was a house afflicted with elephantiasis that one found one had entered, when, having mounted the steps under the porch, having passed through the front door and down the narrow dark passage with its ochre walls and its tessellated floor of magenta and indigo tiles, one looked upwards and saw the staircase twisting steeply up its elongated well – spiralling away into a thin infinitude, until, far above, one's surprised vision came upon a dome of pink and white glass, which yet one judged, with an unerring instinct, was not the top – no, not nearly, nearly the top. Below the ground-floor there was a basement, above it there was a drawing-room floor, and above that there were four floors of bedrooms; so that altogether the house contained seven layers of human habitation. But that was not all; all the rooms were high, but the height of the drawing-room was enormous; so that, if one had the courage to go up the stairs, one found, when one had surmounted the first floor, that one was on an airy eminence, surrounded by immeasurable spaces of yellow marbled wallpaper, and alarmingly near the dome; its pink lights seemed to glitter almost within one's reach, when, abruptly one's course deviated; one turned to the left up six strangely broad steps, and came upon quite a new part of the building – the bedrooms, piled two and two on the top of one another, connected by quite an ordinary, small staircase, and forming a remote, towering outgrowth upon the monstrous structure below.

The house had been designed extraordinarily badly. The rooms that looked on to the street (one on each floor) were tolerable; all the rest were very small and very dark. There was not a scrap of garden, not even a courtyard; and so lugubrious was the outlook of the back rooms that the windows of most of them were of pink and white ground glass, so that one never saw out of them. In a London winter, very little light indeed came through those patterned panes. My mother, taking a hint from my father's office in the City, had 'reflectors' put up – huge plates of glassy material, slightly corrugated, which hung opposite the windows from chains. The windows themselves were so large that it was almost impossible to open them. Little circular ventilators were cut in them, working by means of cords. All this presented a peculiar spectacle, as one sat in the schoolroom – at the end of the passage on the ground-floor – or in 'the young ladies' room', behind the dining-room; a tiny apartment, far higher than it was either long or broad, with a gigantic mahogany door, and the vast window, pink and frosted, with its string and ventilator, and a dim vision of filthy yellow bricks, chains, and corrugations looming through the fog outside.

And besides the height and the darkness there were other strange inconveniences. There was the one and only bath-room, for instance, perched, with its lavatory, in an impossible position midway between the drawing-room and the lowest bedroom floors – a kind of crow's nest – to reach which, one had to run the gauntlet of stairs innumerable, and whose noises of rushing waters were all too audible from the drawing-room below.

Then, in spite of its gigantic size, the house, somehow or other, seemed to have very few rooms in it. My father was the only person who had a sitting-room to himself. In the miserable little 'young ladies' room', Dorothy and Pippa, and Pernel, and later on Marjorie, led an oddly communal existence; privacy there, I suppose occasionally there must have been, but privacy arranged, studied and highly precarious. But, strangest of all, my mother had no room of her own. There was a large writing-table in the dining-room, and at that writing-table, amid the incessant *va-et-vient* of a large family, my mother did all her business – and she was a busy woman, with a multitude of outside interests, a large correspondence, and a curiously elaborate system of household accounts.

No doubt, in all large families, there is very little privacy; and one might say that Lancaster Gate was, in essence, the crowning symbol of the large family system. The one implied the other. The same vitality, the same optimism, the same absence of nerves, which went to the deliberate creation of ten children, built the crammed, high, hideous edifice that sheltered them. And so it was inevitable that the most characteristic feature of the house – its centre, its summary, the seat of its soul, so to speak – should have been the room which was the common meeting-place of all the members of the family – the drawing-room. When one entered that vast chamber, when, peering through its foggy distances, ill-lit by gas-jets, or casting one's eyes wildly towards the infinitely distant ceiling overhead, one struggled to traverse its dreadful length, to reach a tiny chair or a far-distant fireplace, conscious as one did so that some kind of queer life was clustered thick about one, that heaven knows how many eyes watched from just adumbrated sofas, that brains crouched behind the piano, that there were other presences, remote, aloof, self-occupied, and mysteriously dominating the scene – then, in truth, one had come – whether one realized it or no – into an extra-ordinary holy of holies. The gigantic door, with its flowing portière of pale green silk, swung and shut behind one. One stepped forwards in the direction of the three distant windows covered by their pale green limitless curtains, one looked about, one of the countless groups of persons disintegrated, flowed towards one, one sat and spoke and listened: one was reading the riddle of the Victorian Age.

I only mean to say that the Lancaster Gate drawing-room was, in its general nature, the concentrated product of an epoch; for certainly it was too full of individuality and peculiarity to be typical of anything. For one thing, it was too intelligent. I believe that it was not absolutely ugly; the decorations were undoubtedly, for the time, slightly advanced. But it is almost impossible for me to come to an impartial judgement on it. I know it far too well. To the entering stranger, puzzled and alarmed, the impression it produced may well have been one of mere confusion; to me, all was clear, all was articulate, every one of the innumerable details was accurately, intimately, and unforgettably known. At this moment I am perfectly certain that I could reconstruct the whole complexity, complete and exact in every inch. The details were indeed literally innumerable, but there was a climax – immediately obvious – in the arrangement of them. This climax occurred at the more distant of the two mantel-pieces – on the right-hand wall, near the window end of the room – a very large high structure of a most peculiar kind. But I cannot hope to describe that bulk of painted wood with its pilasters and cornices, its jars and niches, its marble and its multi-coloured tiles. Designed by Halsey Ricardo, it com-bined, with an effect of emasculated richness, the inspiration of William Morris, reminiscences of the Renaissance, and a bizarre idiosyncrasy of its own. Guests, finding themselves for the first time face to face with this colossal complication, nearly always exclaimed 'What a magnificent mantelpiece!' It is difficult to see what else they could have done, for to have remained silent before an object so peculiarly conspicuous would have been decidedly marked. Standing by that mottled hearth, one had reached the citadel of the great room. Surveying it from that vantage-spot, one could see that it was a room that was utterly unromantic. It was a mere rectangular parallelepiped – a large ill-shaped box, crammed in between a whole series of exactly similar boxes, ranged on each side of it up and down the street. And yet, though there was no romance in it, there certainly *was* something that was not quite analysable. Was it the effect of its size or its ugliness or its

21

absurdity? – I don't know; but familiar, incredibly familiar as it was to me, who had spent my whole life in it, there was never a time when I was not, in the recesses of my consciousness, a little surprised by it. It was like one of those faces at which one can look for ever without growing accustomed to. Up to my last hour in it, I always felt that the drawing-room was strange.

Strange indeed! Is it conceivable, after all, that I ever was really there? Is it conceivable that Dorothy [Strachey], evening after evening, in that room, kissed me a hundred times, in a rapture of laughter and affection, counting her kisses, when I was six? that, in that same room, perhaps twenty years later, sitting on a sofa alone with Andrew, I suddenly kissed *him*, much to his surprise and indignation – 'My dear man! Really! One doesn't do those things!' – And that – but never mind.

It was a family room – (Andrew, I may mention, was my nephew) – and the family combinations and permutations in it were very various. Apart from the ordinary domestic moments, it was on Sunday afternoons, when my mother was invariably at home, that the family atmosphere, reinforced from without, reached its intensest and its oddest pitch. Then the drawing-room gradually grew thick with aunts and uncles, cousins and connections, with Stracheys, Grants, Rendels, Plowdens, Battens, Ridpaths, Rowes. One saw that it had indeed been built for them – it held them all so nicely, so naturally, with their interminable varieties of age and character and class – from Nina Grey in her faded airs of Roman Catholic aristocracy to Fanny Stanley and her lodging-house garrulity, from Uncle George, bent double with age and eccentricity, hideously sniffing, and pouring out his opinions upon architecture and Tasso to anyone who ventured within his reach, to Black Pat, youthful, horribly snouted, absurdly mendacious, who had come, it was clear, by arrangement, to meet Millie Plowden, and overdid his surprise when at last in yellow feathers she giggled into the room.

The crowd was at its largest at about six, and then it gradually thinned away. But somebody very often stayed on to dinner – Sir William Ward, perhaps, who, besides having been Governor of the Straits Settlements was an executor, of astonishing brilliancy, on the pianoforte. Pressed to play, he would seat himself at the piano and dash into a Chopin waltz with the verve of a high-stepping charger, when suddenly a very odd and discordant sound, rising and falling with the music, would make itself heard. It was something between a snore and a whistle, and nobody could think what it could be. But the mystery was at last explained – the ex-Governor suffered, in moments of excitement, from a curious affection of the nose. While the family listened, a little hysterically, to this peculiar combination of sounds, all at once yet *another* sound – utterly different – burst upon their ears – the sound, this time, of rushing water. There was a momentary shock; and then we all silently realized that someone, in the half-way landing upstairs, was using the w.c.

There are various ways of 'seeing life'; but it seems to me that, in one way or another, I saw a good deal of life in the drawing-room at Lancaster Gate. And of course my experience then was not limited to an enormous family: there was a constant succession of callers, there were repeated dinner-parties and at homes. The preparations for an afternoon party I have a queer vision of – a vision, as it happens, that can be accurately dated. The room was bared, the chairs ranged round the walls, and in the middle, walking up and down and showing themselves off were Dorothy and Pippa dressed from head to foot in white muslin with full flowing skirts, and black satin sashes round their waists, tied in immense bows. They were in mourning – for the death of the German Emperor; and that afternoon party must have been in the third week of June 1888. Often, there were musical parties, and, in the days when trousers were even more unfamiliar to me than they are now, I heard, to my intense excitement, that Grossmith – the almost mythical Grossmith of the *Sorcerer* and the *Pinafore* – was coming to sing and play. 'I know what'll happen,' I whispered to Marjorie, in a great state of agitation, as we waited for the guests. 'Just as Grossmith comes into the room, my knickerbockers will fall down.' The grandest of the musical parties was much later, given in combination by my aunt and my mother, with Joachim and

Piatti playing in their quartet. I can see at this moment, in my mind's eye, the Olympian features of Sir Frederic Leighton, flushed with anger, as he entered on that occasion. I can hear him explaining, in heated accents, that he had made a mistake, had gone to the wrong house, and had been driving over half London in consequence.

It must not be inferred from these entertainments that we were fashionable or smart; on the contrary, if anything we were dowdy; though on the other hand, we were not in the least Bohemian. Our conventionality, slightly mitigated by culture and intelligence, was impinged upon much more seriously by my mother's constitutional vagueness and immateriality, and by a vein in her of oddity and caprice. Her feeling for what was right and proper was unsupported by the slightest touch of snobbery; and, while it was very strong and quite unhesitating, it was surprisingly peculiar to herself. That her daughters should go into mourning for the German Emperor, for instance, appeared to her essential; but her own dresses were most extraordinary, designed by herself, quite regardless of fashion. She had all her children christened, but she never went to Church – except in the country, when she went with the utmost regularity. She was religious in the payment of calls; but the arrangements of the household, from the point of view of social life, were far below the standard. We kept up the mere minimum of an appearance. Our butler, Frederick, the promoted gardener's boy of Stowey House, uncouth, simian, with a great mouth, ill-covered by a straggling moustache, was one of the most unpresentable of figures, and must have cast a chill upon the visitor to whom he opened the door for the first time. 'Why do the Stracheys allow their man to wear a moustache?' Marjorie, in hiding in the dining-room, once heard a military visitor inquire of another as they went down the passage together. Why did they indeed? But in truth my mother would no more have dreamt of ordering the unfortunate Frederick – one of the most excellent of creatures, in spite of his ugliness – to shave off his moustache than she would have dreamt of going without a butler altogether and having a parlour-maid. A butler, but an unpresentable butler, might have stood for the symbol of the Lancaster Gate establishment.

No doubt a contributing cause of our dowdiness was that we were only precariously well off. But, whatever the explanation, I think, as I look back, that the fact that we *were* dowdy was one of the redeeming elements in the situation. Few things could be imagined more terrible than a *smart* Lancaster Gate. As it was, there was something human in the untidyness and the dirt. It was a touch of nature that, in the hall, by the stairs, two bicycles should be grouped together, incompletely covered by a rug, that the dust was too thick on the red velvet in the alcove behind the cast of the Venus of Milo, and that, in the dining-room, my mother's writing-table, littered with papers, stood out obvious and unashamed during the largest dinner-parties. To the children, at any rate, nosing into corners, the full incorrectitude of the place stood revealed. Visitors, perhaps, might not particularly notice, but *we* knew by heart all the camouflaged abysses, taking a sardonic delight in the ruthlessness of the introspective realism with which we plumbed and numbered 'filth-packet' after 'filth-packet' – for such was our too descriptive phrase.

What had happened was that a great tradition – the aristocratic tradition of the eighteenth century – had reached a very advanced stage of decomposition. My father and my mother belonged by birth to the old English world of country-house gentlefolk – a world of wealth and breeding, a world in which such things as footmen, silver, and wine were the necessary appurtenances of civilized life. But their own world was different: it was the middle-class professional world of the Victorians, in which the old forms still lingered, but debased and enfeebled, in which Morris wallpapers had taken the place of Adam panelling, in which the swarming retinue had been reduced to a boy in livery, in which the spoons and forks were bought at the Army and Navy Stores. And then, introducing yet another element into the mixture, there was the peculiar disintegrating force of the Strachey character. The solid bourgeois qualities were interpenetrated by intellectualism and eccentricity. Our family dinners expressed the complicated state of things. They were long and serious meals; but, unless there were visitors, we never dressed for them. At the end, the three mystic bottles of port, sherry, and claret were put at the head of the table and solemnly circulated – the port, sherry and claret having come from the grocer's round the corner. The butler and the liveried boot-boy waited on us, and the butler was Frederick, or, later, a figure even more characteristic of our subtle *dégringolade* – Bastian[i] – a fat, black-haired, Italianate creature, who eventually took to drink, could hardly puff up the stairs from the basement, and, as he handed the vegetables, exuded an odour of sweat and whisky into one's face. He disappeared – after a scene of melodramatic horror – to be replaced by Mr Brooks who, we could only suppose, must have been a groom in earlier life, since all his operations were accompanied by a curious sound of *sotto voce* hissing – or, of course, he might have been Sir William Ward, rather thinly disguised. Peering into the drawers of the sideboard, we discovered tangled masses of soda water-bottle wires, broken corkscrews, napkins, and the mysterious remains of disembowelled brushes. We took note of another filth-packet, observing at the same time, with gusto, that the glass stopper of the brandy decanter had been removed by Mr Brooks, and that a cork had been rammed into its place.

Disintegration and *dégringolade*, no doubt, and yet the total effect, materialized and enormously extended, was of a tremendous solidity. Lancaster Gate towered up above us, and around us, an imperturbable mass – the framework, almost the very essence – so it seemed – of our being. Was it itself, perhaps, one vast filth-packet, and we the mere *disjecta membra* of vanished generations, which Providence was too busy or too idle to clear away? So, in hours of depression, we might have unconsciously theorized; but nevertheless, in reality, it was not so. Lancaster Gate vanished into nothingness, and we survive. To me, that that régime would inevitably, someday, come to an end was a dreadful thought – one not to be dwelt upon – like death; what would, what *could* happen, when we went away from Lancaster Gate? Circumstances – a diminished income – brought about at length the unspeakable catastrophe: but I see now that, whatever had happened, however rich we might have continued, Lancaster Gate was in fact doomed. The disintegration would have grown too strong for it at last. Indeed the end, I think, had really come before we actually left it: Dorothy, with extraordinary courage, married a penurious French artist,[3] and Lancaster Gate was shaken to its foundations. The new spirit was signalized by the omission – under the feeble plea of the difference in nationality – of a wedding service in a church – an omission which would have been impossible ten years earlier; but a family party to celebrate the occasion it was out of the question to omit. Once more the drawing-room was flooded by those familiar figures even Uncle William in his coat and waistcoat of quaint cut and innumerable buttons – the very same that he might have worn in the forties in Holland House – even Mabel Batten, with that gorgeous bust on which the head of Edward the Seventh was wont to repose – were there. When the strange company had departed, something – though at the time we hardly realized it – had happened; it was the end of an age.

The actual events of life are perhaps unimportant. One is born, grows up, falls in love, falls out of love, works, is happy, is unhappy, grows old, and dies – a tedious, a vulgar, succession; but not there lies the significance of a personal history: it is the atmosphere that counts. What happened to me during my first twenty-five years of consciousness may well be kept to the imagination; what cannot be left to the imagination is the particular, and amazing, web on which the pattern of my existence was woven – in other words, Lancaster Gate. To imagine *that*! – To reconstruct, however dimly, that grim machine, would be to realize with some distinctness the essential substance of my biography. An incubus sat upon my spirit, like a cat on a sleeping child. I was unaware, I was unconscious, I hardly understood that anything else could be. Submerged by the drawing-room, I inevitably believed that the

[3] In 1903 Dorothy Strachey married Simon Bussy. As Dorothy Bussy she became well-known for her translations of André Gide. She was also the author of *Olivia* by 'Olivia' (1949).

drawing-room was the world. Or rather, I neither believed nor disbelieved; it *was* the world, so far as I was concerned. Only, all the time, I did dimly notice that there was something wrong with the world – that it was an unpleasant shape.

Of course, it would be absurd to pretend that I was permanently and definitely unhappy. It was not a question of unhappiness so much as of restriction and oppression – the subtle unperceived weight of the circumambient air. And there were moments, luckily, when some magic spring within me was suddenly released, and I threw off that weight, my spirit leaping up into freedom and beatitude. Coming home in the night in the summer once from the Temple with Clive,[4] parting from him, excited, faintly amorous, opposite the sentry at St James's Palace, walking on in the early morning opalescence through sleeping Mayfair and down the Bayswater Road, where the County Council carts were sprinkling the pavements with pale blue disinfectant water – I arrived at last at number 69, a little weary, but not too weary to face with equanimity the long climb that lay in front of me before I reached my bed. Up and up I went, curling round the great dim ochre well, round and up, until the dome loomed over me, and, looking over the banisters, I hung high in mid space, then turned, went up the six broad steps, then passed bedroom after bedroom, up and up still, leaving the nursery floor behind me, until I reached the bedroom, which, for the moment, was mine – almost at the very top of the house – at the back – overlooking, from an incredible height, a mews and roof and chimneys. I opened the door and went in, and immediately saw that the second bed – there was invariably a second bed in every bedroom – was occupied. I looked closer: it was Duncan;[5] and I was not surprised: he had lingered on, no doubt, till it was too late to go home, and had been provided with the obvious accommodation. I undressed, oddly exultant, in the delicious warm morning. As I was getting into bed I saw that all the clothes had

---

[4] Clive Bell, the art critic.
[5] Duncan Grant, Strachey's cousin, was the son of Lady Strachey's brother Bartle.

rolled off Duncan – that he was lying, almost naked, in vague pyjamas – his body – the slim body of a youth of nineteen – exposed to the view. I was very happy; and, smiling to myself, I wondered why it was that I did not want – not want in the very least – what the opportunity so perfectly offered, and I got into bed, and slept soundly, and dreamt no prophetic dreams.

June 1922

2

DURING THE SUMMER holidays, Strachey would escape from
the awful oppression of Lancaster Gate when his mother took
her children up to The Doune, her family home in
Rothiemurchus. In July and August this house was packed
often with the whole Strachey tribe, in addition to the Grants,
Strachey's first cousins. Amid the massive and imposing
landscape, the pine forests and open skies, Strachey passed
some of the happiest days of his childhood, fishing, vaulting
streams, playing cricket and robbers, and scaling the slopes of
the Cairngorms. In contrast to the crowded and claustro-
phobic atmosphere of London, it was an outdoor sunlit life,
dissolving the mists of illness and pessimism, into which he
emerged like a butterfly liberated from its chrysalis.

Rothiemurchus continued to hold a significance for Strachey
all his life. He would often return there, especially during
periods of unhappiness, for in these surroundings he seemed
able to recapture the sensations of long ago, escape adult
complexities, and return to the best days of his youth. 'The
days of childhood, with their passionate pains and pleasures,
are with us,' he wrote to Lumsden Barkway while staying
there in 1899; 'days nearer to us, too, with their precious
moments of bitterness and love; and the present day that is
fading beneath the hills for ever ... Here, among the
mountains, the Vision of Balliol itself seems to dwindle and
appear insignificant.' In this way, Rothiemurchus eased his
self-dissatisfaction, the beauties of Nature compensating for
the lack of beauty he sometimes found unendurable in

31

humanity. After each stay there he felt fortified. 'This place is, qua place, perfection,' he told Virginia Stephen (24 August 1908), '—one begins to realize in it that Nature may be romantic and beautiful. I linger by lakes, and tear up mountains all day long.' And to his mother he confessed that the country was so 'divine' that 'I feel I shall never be able to tear myself away from it'.

Strachey's schooling, which turned out unconventionally, was arranged for him by his mother. In 1889 he was sent to a tiny school run by a Mr Henry Forde at Parkstone, on Poole Harbour in Dorset. Here he could combine the benefits of private coaching with those of Victorian sea-air. His health and scholarship remained moderate, but he stayed at Parkstone until the summer of 1893.

DIARY OF GILES LYTTON STRACHEY IN THE SUMMER HOLIDAYS OF 1890, 1891

Mon 28th July 1890

We started for Scotland at 8 p.m. from King's Cross. I came up with Dorothy, Pippa and Pernie.[1] We arrived at York at 12 p.m. and ate sandwiches.

Tue 29th July 1890

We arrived at Perth at 7 a.m. (an hour late). We met Pat[2] there. And all started for Aviemore at 9.25 a.m. We had breakfast at Perth. We arrived at Aviemore at 1 p.m. In the afternoon Pat and I played on the grass and had some strawberrys &c &c.

Wen 30th July 1890

Mama, Marjorie,[3] Jembeau & I went in the carriage to Aunt Minnie and walked back by the Spey. In the afternoon we had cricket.

---

[1] Dorothy, Pippa (Philippa) and Pernie (Joan Pernel) were Lytton's sisters.
[2] Patrick Grant was Lytton's cousin, the son of Charles Grant and elder brother of Lady Strachey. Another brother, George, also had a son called Pat – 'White Pat' as he was nicknamed. White Pat was presumed by the family to be a good character, and Black Pat a bad one, until, years later, White Pat ran off with Black Pat's wife.
[3] Marjorie was Lytton's younger sister, and Jembeau (James Beaumont) his younger brother.

Thu 31st July 1890

Mama, Pernie, Marjorie Jembeau and I went to the kitchen
garden and had three strawberrys each. Directly after dinner
Uncle Bartle and Aunt Ethel went away. In the morning Pat
and I rode on the pony. In the afternoon Mama and I went to
Loch An Eilan we were caught in a shower and had to go in to
Mrs Grant. As we were going back we went into Mrs Mitchel.
After that we met all the others and Marjorie went back with
us we called on the Miss Martineaus and went round their
garden then we had cricket with the Fosters.

Fri 1st August 1890

Mama, Dodo, Pernie and I went to the church yard. In the
afternoon we went to the school treat where we had great fun
with Aunt Minnie and Sarah.

Sat 2nd August 1890

We all went with Naomi and cousin Sidney to Loch Morlich
except Mama and Marjorie who went to the Lochans. I caught
one fish and Cousin Sidney caught five. We had dinner on the
shore. As we were driving to the door Oliver[4] appeared to our
great surprise.

Sun 3rd August 1890

Oliver and I played with the peacock. We all went to church at
12 a.m. It rained in the afternoon. In the evening Oliver and
Marjorie and I played with the peacock. Mama read some Iliad
in the afternoon.

Mon 4th August 1890

We played cricket. Pernie and Pat went to meet Marrion and
Maggie in the afternoon Oliver and I played with the Peacock.
In the evening we played on combs and Papa came.

[4] Oliver was an elder brother of Lytton's.

Tue 5th August 1890

We played on the grass. In the afternoon we had cricket with Maggie and Naomi. In the evening we had Musical chairs and Dumbcrambo. Aunt Lelle came in the afternoon. Mama read some Iliad.

Wen 6th August 1890

We played the Rober Band all the afternoon. In the morning Pat and I went to the Dynamo.

Thu 7th August 1890

We played at Rober Band. In the afternoon we all went to the station in the carriage and Oliver and I bought whistles. We met Maggie there who walked back with Pernie we meet Nurse and Jembeau, who came back with us. Maggie and Naomi came and Uncle Charlie photographed us.

Fri 8th August 1890

We played on the grass. Dodo read The Abbot. In the afternoon Mama read the Iliad.

Sat 9th August 1890

We all went (except Duncan and James) to Alt Dru where we had lunchion Pippa, Dodo, Aunt Aggie and Uncle Charlie started earlier and went up Brae Reach. Pat and Oliver fished with Cousin Sidney (who came too) Mamma showing Mags and me how to jump with a pole sprained her ankle but made it all wright by putting it in the stream. Naomi's hat and mine fell into the water.

Sun 10th August 1890

The others went to church and I stayed at home. In the

afternoon Mama read some Iliad. Oliver and Pernie scetched Maggie came to tea.

Mon 11th August 1890

Oliver Per[n]ie and I scetched. In the afternoon Papa, Mama Marjorie and I went up Ord Baen (Oliver and Pernie went up another way) we came down by Loch an Eilan where the carriage fetched us.

Tue 12th August 1890

It rained all day Charlie came in the afternoon. We danced in the afternoon. Oliver went back with Charlie to the Boathouse and had dinner there.

Wen 13th August 1890

We went to the station (that is to say Oliver Pernie and I) coming back Naomi saw us and Pernie stayed to lunchion, we stayed at the Boathouse and Charlie played on the Bagpipes.

END OF PART I

Mon 27th July 1891

I arrived at Lancaster Gate from Mr Forde's at 12.30 p.m. In the afternoon Papa and I went to his office and then went to the Royal Naval Exhibition. We first saw a little fight on the lake and three Red Flags were put in the middle of the Lake and were blown up by a torpedeau. Then we saw a panorama of the Battle of Trafalgar and a model of the Victory (life size). There was Nelson (done in waxworks and several other people bending over him. After that we saw all the Armstrong guns &c. One of which was a hundred & ten ton gun. I had some shots at bouys passing with a smaller gun and hit once and missed five times! Then we saw the Iceburg which was rather foolish it consisted of a ship in some false ice and a few men pulling a sledge along. A little speech was made about the seasons of the Polar year and it got dark and light alternatly and the Araura Borealis appeared. Then, we had dinner—. Then we saw all the models &c &c. Then we went to the Lake and saw the night battle the whole place was lighted up with electric light which looked very pretty. There were fire-works continualy and Two Big Torpedeau boats banged as the forts banged back. Then we came home.

Tue 28th July 1891

I went to Rose Paul for luncheon – because Papa had gone to the city and all the others had gone to Scotland on the 20th – After Luncheon Rose and I went from Glouster Road Station (underground) to Victoria, where Papa met us and we all went to the Crystal Palace. The first thing we saw was 'The Wonderful Performance of Wild Beasts'. There were twelve lions & three tigers, two chetas, two bears one black and the other was a polar bear, and there were three dogs who were meant, I think to keep the others in order and I think the beasts were given something to make them insensable as they looked very drowsy. The best trick they did was this – a chariot was brought and Tigers were harnessed to it and a lion got in and a crown was put on his head and a red robe over his back and they drove round & round several times. Then we had dinner. After that we saw a little play called The Witch's haunt which was very pretty, then we came home. We saw The Panorama of The Battle of Metz between Dinner and The Beasts, and went in aerial Flight, it was a little sort of boat with about five seats, only wide enough to hold two people on each and was hung up by a rope and pulled by a wire over a pond. It was rather alarming!

Wen 29th July 1891

I went to Rose Paul in the morning and found Lila there. Lila & I played at dominoes after luncheon Rose read to us, and at four o'clock Cousin Minnie came in a carriage and took us all to Westminster Abbey and then took Lila to the station and Rose saw her off. Then we went back to Rose's. After Papa came and took us to the Nautch Girl (a play) which was very nice. After that we dropped Rose at her house and came home.

3

ALTHOUGH HENRY FORDE *reported that Strachey 'eats with capital appetite' and had done some 'spirited painting', Lady Strachey was disappointed by his persistent bouts of ill-health, fearing that they would set him so far back with his work that he would not be able to pass the entrance examination for a public school. She therefore arranged for him a five-month recuperative cruise, so that, while avoiding the worst of the English winter, he might benefit from greater quantities of sea-air.*

The diary in which he recorded the adventures and amusements of this journey was his most ambitious literary work to date. It was probably written at the suggestion of his mother as a means of keeping up his 'English Composition'. His geography was certain to be improved, and as for other subjects, his elder sister Dorothy (then a schoolmistress in Wimbledon) could give him a little private tuition.

On his return to Parkstone in June 1893 Henry Forde wrote to Lady Strachey:

He certainly does look grown in every way: his cheeks are quite plump. I am rather surprised to see that he is not at all tanned by the suns and seas of his journey. He bears his return to humdrum work and life like the philosophical boy he is; set to at his Virgil this morning as if he had only left off the day before, and is taking the ovation the boys are giving him – and which seems likely to continue for days, like a Roman Triumph – with dignity and as if it too were quite in its place and to be expected, and altogether is possessing his soul in blandness and calm. He is a most admirable boy.

DIARY OF G. L. STRACHEY

Friday Dec 23rd 1892

Shortly after Mama had left, as Dorothy and I were walking on the deck, we heard yells from the shore; we went to see what was the matter and found that it was a female in apparent histerics. Soon after we saw her boxes being taken off the ship. A little time after we had started there was rather a comotion on board, as the ship was blocked on all sides and could not pass. At last however we managed to get through all right into the lock – we soon were out speeding towards the Channel. We had dinner at half past six and sat at a side table. I sat at the corner nearest the port and Dorothy next me (on my right), next her sat a young man called Parry. At the end of the table was a young man called d'Alton he went in for being funny, he is very short and small, dark, with a *very* curly moustachio which he twirled with pride, he sings and plays well. Parry told Dodo all his private history, viz: that his parents had died and that he and his brother thought this was a good opportunity of taking a two years trip round the world. It was bitterly cold all day and we all huddled round the fire, one gent told anecdotes to pass away the time. Dodo wrote a letter to Mama and then we both went to bed, as we were going there I felt as if we were in the channel – which we were!

Saturday Dec 24th

Woke up in the morning and the stewardess brought me some

tea and biscuits. I remained in my berth all day and was all right in the morning but worse in the afternoon. I was slightly sick in the evening and had some champaigne. There are two stories about the female on the shore; some say that the captain saw her swigging off whiskey and soda, and that he turned her off the ship; others say that she was being forced to go to meet her husband and that she refused to go. I slept quite well on Friday night.

Sunday Dec 25th

Had a good night and remained in bed all day, as long as I lay still all was well, but directly I sat up I began to feel bad. It was Christmas day but I did not partake of Turkey or Plum Pudding! It was rough all day (in the bay).

Monday Dec 26th

Slept well. Steward said we would be round Cape Finistere by half past two, and that then we should have beautiful weather, so we ditermined to get up after luncheon. At three I got out of bed and felt very bad and was violently sick, after that I felt much better and managed to get on half my clothes amongst which a pair of knickers. I then collapsed on to my berth where I lay in a heap. Dorothy had by this time dressed and was up on deck. I stayed on my berth for about a quarter of an hour (it seemed to me) and then Dodo came in and said 'you must get up, its simply lovely on deck' and she put on my greatcoat and I staggered up. When I was up I sank into a chair and looked about me – How lovely everything was – the sea and sky were blue – the sun was shining – the air was fresh – everything was delicous! No one would have thought it was the 26th Dec! Presently the thought came into my head that I would have to go down below sometime or other, which thought was odious! We went down for the chicken course for dinner and then came up again and stayed up till we returned to bed (I got in with all speed).

Tuesday Dec 27th

Got up after breakfast and went on deck where I waited for
Dorothy for about an hour and a half and passed the time by
eating an apple. The day passed quickly and it was very calm,
nothing particular happened, it was very fine and nice all day.
Saw Spain today.

Wednesday Dec 28th

We were supposed to arrive at Gibraltar at about 12 in the
morning. There was a lovely view of the coast of Spain – really
very pretty. We could also see Africa, it was not quite so nice.
We passed a little Spanish town with a lighthouse and convent.
At last we got within view of Gibraltar, it looked very funny as
if it was an island only as you come nearer, you could see it was
connected to the mainland by a long sandy spit – about 700
yards long. It looked something like this—

Gibraltar from the sea.

The leftermost hill is really the highest and the thing on the top
is the signal station. The rightermost thing is Europa Point
with a lighthouse on top. Our house is in the middle hill. It
began to drizzle at half past eleven but left off when we arrived.
I went forward and saw the boxes being hauled out of the hold
by a steam crane. By the time we had stopped, with the aid of
spectacles, I could see what the place looked like. All the
houses were like toy houses scatered about the rock and to
complete the smallness, the water became filled with little toy

boats (at any rate compared with the Coromandel they were) which came to take passengers to the shore. We collected our baggage satisfactorily, and in a few minutes, we saw Uncle Charlie's[1] tall figure ascending the steps into the ship. After a little fuss we and our boxes were sitting in a boat, being rowed to land. When we got there we found Pat waiting on the quay. We then got into a cab (a very ramshackle affair) it was quite open and jerked violently it looked like a four post bed (not only this particular one, but every one). Soon got to the house, where Aunt Aggie was. Pat and I sleep together in a very nice, large room. The house is two stories high and has a view of the Bay. There are lots of roses and heaps of 'Pokers', large red flowers with long stalks. There are oranges growing everywhere but very small. In the afternoon, as Pat had been invited to a party I went with him. It was in a church! and there was a Christmas tree. It was most curious, and given by the scotch minister. We sat in the pews, and were given presents. Pat was given a sort of purse and pocket book combined and I was presented with a box of chocolates. We came home in a cab.

Thursday Dec 29th

Pat and I went to the Alameda (the public gardens) and looked at the great guns there, (they looked very formidable) they were painted the same colour as the grass or earth around them so as not to be seen by the enemy. In the afternoon we played bezique. It was very fine all day. The Piper came today.

Friday Dec 30th

Dodo, Pat and I went to the town and then came back again! Aunt Aggie went to see the Point to point race in which the Royal Engineers won. In the afternoon Pat and I climbed trees. We went to town because Dodo wanted to return some books to the library. The piper is called Smith, he teaches me the fling.

---

[1] Uncle Charlie was Charles Grant, the father of Black Pat, who accompanied Lytton on most of this journey. Aunt Aggie was his wife.

As I look out of my window I see, through Olive trees and various others, the blue bay dotted with many ships of different kinds, and beyond it I see the mountains of Spain, the far off ones of a half grey, half pale blue tint, and the nearer ones green. On the sides of these mountains I see white towns, small and pretty. And then above the mountains is the blue, blue sky – without a cloud – without a thing to mar its beauty, and in the midst of it the sun is shining brightly and pouring its heat upon me. Everything adds to make the scene most beautiful.

Saturday Dec 31st

It rained all the morning and we invented a game called Stocks. In the afternoon Pat and I went to Windmill flats where we could see the Mediterranean dimly as it was drizzling. Nothing more happened today.

Sunday 1st Jan

Aunt Aggie, Dodo, Pat and I went to Windmill Flats and then round Europa Point home, the Mediterranean was a beautiful blue, it was a lovely day and felt like Sunday in the Summer in Hyde Park. There is a little house facing the Mediterranean in which the Governor resides in the summer as it is too hot in his other house, it is called the Govenor's Cottage, there are exquisite pokers in the garden. When we got to Europa Pt there was the Mediterranean on the left and the Atlantic on the right. You could not see a line separating them down the middle strange to say. We did not go to church in the morning as it was wet. Our walk in the afternoon was very nice.

Monday 2nd Jan

Today is the Children's dance given by the Govenor. Pat and I are going. In the afternoon I got my hair cut and bought some white gloves. The town has narrow streets and is rather dirty in some places. The people in the streets are chiefly soldiers or town-criers. At last the wished for time arrives. Mrs Grogan (next door neighbour) takes us in her cab as she is taking two of her children (called Aileen and Gerald) Aileen is the eldest (12 years old) and is a great friend of ours. Gerald is 8½ and is young for his age. But to return to the dance, we arrived at the Convent (Govenors house) and took off our things. I had on Etons with best trousers and black tie and white kid gloves and rose button-hole (not like Olivers!) The ballroom is very nice and large and I hopped round it. I was introduced to a female 3 times! The worst of it was she was hideous! I enjoyed myself greatly and came back at about 12.

Tuesday 3rd Jan

Remained in bed, both of us till 10! In the afternoon Aileen Pat and I went to Old Man's Garden it is a little way up the rock, we went to get flowers for the dinner party Aunt Aggie was going to give. We could not get many. It was very hot. Pat and I had dinner in our room. Aunt Aggie and Dodo went to a ball afterwards.

Wednesday 4th Jan

Uncle Charlie got a pass to go up the rock. They are very particular as to who you take, so we thought we would have to invent a story as Meadows was coming too. Uncle Charlie said it ought to be Pat & I the two sons and Dodo & Meadows our wives! At about three we started it was a lovely day and very hot. After we had gone a little way the path was blocked by barbed wire. And it was with great difficulty that the fair sex got over it. This difficulty once got over, we continued our journey satisfactorily it was very hot work getting up but at last we reached the summit I picked some narcissus on the way, it was lovely. There is a little house in the Signal Station, it is not the highest point on the Rocks. Ropes go down from the Signal Station into the town and up these by means of machinery come baskets with orders and provisions and sometimes soldiers! Once it got stuck with a soldier inside and they had to send up oil to him to oil the wheels! And at last he got down all right! A beautiful view from the Signal Station of both sides of the rock. On the Mediterranean side there is a little fishing village that looks very nice. It is a steep precipice down to the shore. One can also see the neutral ground and the queen of Spain's Chair (a mountain where the queen of Spain reviewed the seige and said she wouldn't leave it till Gibraltar fell). There was an excellent telescope up there it was simply splendid and you could see their dogs in a Spanish Town several miles away! We trudged back and Dodo got tired of going down hill! At last we reached the bottom and got into a cab and drove home. I enjoyed myself very much but was tired.

Saturday 14th Jan

I skip a week of rain and begin, now it has slightly improved. Only *slightly*. Today we are to go round the galleries so we have dinner at one, and start immediately after. We go in a cab to the old Moorish Castle, it is on the other side of the town. You're allowed to see the galleries if you go with an officer in uniform, so Uncle Charlie had to go in his. The Master gunner showed us over them. He talked the whole time and never listened to what anybody said! The galleries are all blasted out of the rock. They are like passages with windows for guns to poke through some of them are very dark and you can't see where you're going. The whole time water keeps on dripping from the top. There are hardly any guns in them, but plenty of places to put them in. Through one of these there is a lovely view of the neutral ground and the Gates of Gibraltar, and also of the causeway between Gib and neutral ground. It is so arranged that at any moment it may be blown up and then it would be impossible to reach Gibraltar by land as the North Front is a mere precipice. We could not go to St George's Chapel which is the most interesting place as no one is allowed to see it except officers. We saw officers quarters in time of siege, they are awful little places in the rock. There is a lovely view of the Bay with all its ships on its blue waters and the beautiful blue sky above. The galleries were most interesting and must have been a pretty hard thing to make. It took three quarters of an hour to go through them. We drove back into the town. Meadows walked home and Uncle Charlie went to the library. And Pat, Aunt Aggie, Dodo and I drove into Linea, the Spanish town just on the other side of the neutral ground. As we drove through this (neutral) we saw smugglers filling their clothes with tobacco because they get it in free here and try to smuggle it over into Spain where there are enormous dutys and try to pass the Spanish sentrys in the night. We saw one woman putting things in her stockings! When we got into Spain a soldier poked his head into the cab to see if it was all right. We were going to see the bull-ring which is in the middle of the town and looks like a small colosseum from a little way off. The streets of Linea are simply too filthy, all the dirt is thrown into the street a gutter runs through the middle and you think the cab is going to capsize every minute, if it did it would be awful! It is simply one pool of dirty mud! The houses look very clean inside. When we got to the bull-ring an old woman came out and showed us over it the cabman came too and acted as interpreter as the old woman could not speak one word of English. Pat had been there before and she recognised him. She showed us the little spears they throw at the bull and a medicine chest for the wounded. The bull is put into a dark stable, and they pull up the doors from above, and directly it sees the light it rushes out into the arena. Inside the bull-ring consists of a round space in the middle, with grass, and seats going up and up and up to the top. The woman said it held 10,000, but John (the cabman) said it was really 1,000. She said she had seen a bullfight once but that she would never see it again – it was too horrible! (John said he had seen seven last year!) There is always a priest to give absolution if necessary. When we went away she gave us a paper with pictures of bull-fights on it. We drove through the piggy streets to the market, which is a very nice one and then home. The bull ring was *most* interesting, and I enjoyed myself immensely the whole of that day. John is the regimental cabman and is half Spanish, half English.

Sunday 15th Jan

Pat and I went to church for the first time. A very short service.

Monday 16th Jan

This is the day the grown-ups are going to Spain. After a lot of fussing it is discovered the boat starts at 3.30 at least they had to be on board at that time. Started from this house at twenty to four and got to the 'ragged staff' at 4 o'clock. The ragged staff is the place they start from. They were in plenty of time as the captain was not yet on board! It was rather cold and windy. We bid them adieu and they rowed off to the steamer. Pat and I walked home. Their boat started at five. Gerald Grogan came to tea and Aileen came afterwards. We played card games.

Tuesday 17th Jan

Very fine but cold in the morning. Went over to the Grogan's after supper. Saw some companys of the Black Watch march past.

Wednesday 18th Jan

Very fine but cold in the morning did nothing particular. The grown-ups return on Monday. The other day saw the 42nd marching up the rock, the whole regiment. They looked very nice as they went past. Uncle Charlie went up without having his breakfast! Am going over to the Grogan's after supper.

Thursday 19th Jan

After breakfast as Pat and I were sitting in the drawing room, we were startled by a great boom of a gun it was *very* loud and all the windows shook and rattled. We went out on to the verandah with telescopes and spectacles to see if we could see anything. We could see the target it was in the sea some way out. We waited and waited for it to boom again, but nothing occurred for a long time. It was so hot and nice out there, that we began sticking in our stamps when all of a sudden there was another tremendous crash and we saw the water spout up into a fountain of spray where the shot touched the water, and then there was a sort of low grumble which was the shot flying over the water, and then there was another splash and another grumble and another splash and another grumble which gradually died away. It went a great distance. The gun was in the Alameda and they were practising. It went on all day and they always got pretty close to the target. Pat and I have bullfights every morning, we squat on the ground and charge against each other, they are very amusing. Directly after luncheon Meadows, Pat and I went off in a cab to Catalan Bay. It is the other side of the rock and there is a little tiny fishing village there on the shores of the Mediterranean. The sea was simply exquisite, a dark blue colour, and it dashed up against the rock and rebounded in a mass of silvery spray. We walked past the little village and up a sand hill on the other side, where we sat on some rocks and watched the sea beneath. There was an old man close by fishing with a bamboo. After some time he caught a beautiful fish about one foot six long, then killed it and put [it] in a nitch in the rock, then he put some sardines on his hook for bait and began fishing again. He was so pleased with his success that he began smoking a cigar. Soon afterwards he caught another and then we had to go as we had been there a good time. It was very nice sitting there watching the waves break on the rocks and the seagulls flying round. We stopped at the North Front to see the football match. It was between the 42nd and 60th Rifles. The 42nd won. We walked home having enjoyed ourselves greatly.

Friday 20th Jan

In the afternoon Meadows, Pat and I walked down to Europa lighthouse to see if we would be allowed to go over it. Europa lighthouse is at the very southernmost point in Gibraltar. When we got there we asked a man who was in a cottage close by if we could see the lighthouse, but he said that the keepers weren't at home but that you were allowed to see it any day of the week. So we resolved to come again tomorrow. Walked home by Windmill Flats.

Saturday 21st Jan

Major Grogan said that there was going to be a Brigade Review today at the North Front. So Meadows, Pat, Aileen and I drove off in a cab thither. When we got to the Alameda we saw the 42nd just starting and we could not get in front of them and had to keep behind them for some time. They looked so nice going through the town, filling up the street from one side to the other. Their white helmets looked like a long white serpent winding along the street. At last we passed them and got to the North Front (opposite to Spain and rather cold). The Middlesex were there and then came the Black Watch and the band was in the middle, we stood behind the band, there were also the Somerset and the Rifles. We thought we were in too bad a position so we walked round to just opposite where we were before. After a little the Govenor appeared, riding, accompanied by his aides de camp, also on horseback. The band then struck up and he (the Gov.) reviewed the men. 1st picture is the first position. He went twice round them, once in front and then behind and then he stood where 2nd picture shows, the bands of all the regiments joined together and formed a square as shown in 2nd picture. Then the regiments marched past in the direction of the arrow. First the Pioneers of all the regiments, then the signal men and then the Middlesex with the Colonel leading and the companies following led by their captain as he passed the Govenor he saluted him with his sword and the Govenor touched his hat. It was very pretty to see the red coats marching past while the band was playing a stirring march and one could hear the tramp, tramp of the soldiers' feet on the ground. The Middlesex and the Somerset have passed and it is the Black Watch who are now approaching. The bagpipes begin to play and the 42nd march past. How lovely they look with their kilts and white feet. Colonel Brickenden and Major Grogan are leading on horseback and the companies follow after them. They stream on and on and I am thinking they will never stop when the adjoutant appears and I know there are no more to follow as he always rides behind the regiment. Then come the Rifles, they look rather dingy compared with the Black Watch, the former being much blacker than the later and very smart. When these have passed after a little fussing the whole crew march back again in the opposite direction, quick time (the bagpipes did not play when 42nd passed). I forgot to say that these carried their colours, very old and covered with holes. The Govenor made a speech which we could not hear, and that was the end of the review. It was a lovely sight and I wouldn't have missed it for worlds. Walked half way back and drove the rest. In the afternoon Meadows, Pat and I walked to the lighthouse, we were shown over it by the keeper. After going up about 80 steps we came to the room where the keepers sit, it looked very comfortable. Ten steps above that was the room in which the lamp is, it is a large one, with two round wicks one inside the other and all round it is thick plate glass, curved like a magnifying glass so as to magnify the light from the lamp. The walls of the room are all glass and it is *very* hot inside. The keeper said that the heat of the sun cracked the glass. There is a piece of red glass to throw a red light on a sunken rock and as the red light is only half as powerful as the white, there is a red reflector throwing red light on the rock as well. The lighthouse was very interesting and well worth seeing. Walked home.

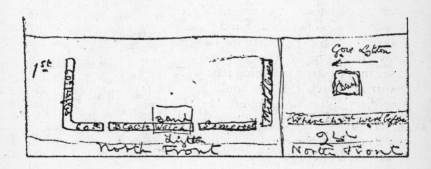

Sunday 22nd Jan

Went to church in the morning and had luncheon and dinner
with the Grogans who are always very kind to us.

Monday 23rd Jan

I forgot to mention we had received postcards from Dodo and
Aunt Aggie to say they were coming home by Algeciras and
that we could come and meet them. Algeciras is the Spanish
town on the other side of the bay. So at 3 o'clock Meadows Pat
and I drove off to the Waterport (one of the quays) and then
got into a rowing boat and rowed off to the Elvira, the little
steamer that goes across to Algeciras. Soon after we were on
board she started and in about twenty minutes we were across.
We then got into another rowing boat and were soon in Spain.
A young Spaniard showed us the way to the railway station.
Their train was to arrive at 4.45 so we had about three quarters
of an hour to wait. We walked about in the town to see what it
was like it was smelly but not *half* so bad as Linea. Outside the
town it is quite country. A lovely day sun blazing and
everything and everybody enjoying themselves. We came back
to the station and walked up and down the platform – the
whole town walked up and down the platform it was evidently
the thing to do. It is past 4.45 – it is past 5 o'clock and yet they
come not. We wait and wait. The sun sinks behind those
beautiful hills – so blue – so high. It is getting cold and still they
come not. We have waited an hour and everyone has gone
except those who occupy seats. We are getting tired we cannot
sit down! What shall we do? Some one sees smoke! Is it the
train? Alas it is only a cottage chimney! It is past six and – at
last – at last they come! The train rolls into the station and they
step out. Dorothy Aunt Aggie, Uncle Charlie all are there. We
are soon in the Elvira speeding towards Gibraltar which looks
very pretty with all the lights of its houses shining. The reason
they did not come earlier was that the engine was rather feeble
and didn't dare go fast.

Tuesday 24th Jan

After tea as Pat and I were sitting in the dining room, we heard Aunt Aggie's voice saying 'Have you heard the news? No, what! the Black Watch are going to be sent to Egypt! We were very surprised at this. I knew that there had been a fuss in Egypt. Aunt Aggie said that most likely we should go on to the Cape that way.

Wednesday 25th Jan

All yesterday Uncle Charlie had been on guard at the North Front. He came back this morning at about eleven. Colonel Brickenden had received 3 telegrams. No one knew what the third was, but it had the effect of making the Colonel smile which most likely meant we were going to stay at Egypt, as the Colonel did not want the regiment to separate at Mauritius. Uncle Charlie thought that if we did go to Egypt we would stay there some months. I was sorry for this as I wanted to go to the Cape. Aunt Aggie was glad. In the afternoon it was announced that the 42nd were to become part of the army of occupation in Egypt!

Thursday 26th Jan

Heard many different reports concerning Egypt. As the luggage had to be on board the Himalaya on Friday, we had to go to a hotel today. Walked down to the Royal in the afternoon, it is in the town.

Friday 27th Jan

Uncle Charlie said the Himalaya had arrived. Meadows, Pat and I walked down to the market by the lime wall several feet thick where we saw the Himalaya she is white and looked very pretty. We then walked towards the Alameda and were nearly there when an orderly stopped us and said that women and children had to be on board today. At this moment Uncle Charlie drove past in a cab, we hopped in and the orderly gave him the order. We all drove to the Royal Hotel. There was rather a fuss getting everything ready. We thought we would start at three but it was put off till five. Dorothy and I walked about the town and she bought some Photos one of which she gave to me. We then went to the Hallam Pass but they were not at home so we had tea in library and then went to the hotel. Soon after Pat and Aunt Aggie arrived they had been paying calls. Then after about half an hour's fuss and bother we succeeded in driving off. I left off when we had driven away from the Royal Hotel. In about a quarter of an hour we stopped and got out. There was a great gate in front of us which had to be opened before we could get to the Himalaya, so a man with a large bunch of keys tried to open it, at least it sounded like a large bunch of keys from the rattling that ensued we could not see exactly as it was rather dark and the gate was a little way off. Then another man went to see if he could open it, and then another and another until there was a crowd collected round the gate. And then ten Middlesex soldiers appeared and fussed about but no effect was produced then Aunt Aggie went to see what was happening and then Pat. Aunt A. returned and said they had opened a little door and as our boxes were not too big they could get them through all right. To make matters worse Uncle Charlie was on baggage gard. A sergeant was sent to fetch him and he soon appeared. He had no more to do so we walked through the little door towards the Himalaya the soldiers carried our baggage. The Himalaya is between four and five thousand tons she looked beautiful as we approached her. We went on board my home for – how long? ah! that is the question! the three grown-ups are going to dinner with the Lakes there to meet Capt. Chichester of the Himalaya so Meadows, Pat and I are left on board. I forgot to mention that we were supposed to sleep in the nursery however when the bedroom steward saw us he said we were much to big, but that we would have to sleep there that night and that he would make, if possible, other arrangements later. Also no one under sixteen is allowed to dine in the saloon so it was arranged we should have supper afterwards. As Pat and I were standing on deck the steward appeared and said by special request we were to have dinner in the Saloon so we rushed and sat down in the midst of Lancashire subalterns, we conversed with a few of them who seemed to think we were going to stay in Egypt.

Saturday

We depart today at one. Before we go simply swarms of people come to see us off especially artillery, the ship was crammed. The Middlesex band was on the quay and played tunes just before we started every one was very kind to Dorothy and they all wanted to see her off as her boat started the next day. The Hallan Pass offered first and were accepted Auld Lang Syne was played and we started Dorothy waving from the shore. Went down and had dinner with the babies. When we came up on deck again we had a lovely view of Gibraltar, the side facing East, where Catalan Bay is, and on we glided through the Mediterranean. Adieu Gibraltar! Adieu! When shall I see you again – who can tell? You have disappeared, O fair Gibraltar, and every minute I am further away from you! Tonight we sleep in Pandemonium, in a good cabin with two subalterns – Harvey and Middleton – Harvey of the 42nd who has come out in a draft from England and Middleton of another regiment. Pat and I are allowed to have our meals with the grown ups and dine in the Saloon. The general regime is as follows: get up at 7.15 a.m. breakfast at 8.30 – 9 a.m. on Deck. Prayers at 10 a.m. to 10.30 (first sailors' then soldiers') Sit on deck till 12. when we have luncheon. After luncheon play quoits. Tea 4.30. Then play quoits till 5.45. Then dress for dinner. 6.30 dinner. 7.45 come on deck – band plays and we dance. 8.45 To bed! If we do not play quoits we read. It gets cold in the evenings, but is very warm in the middle of the day. One day Mr Dick Cunningham wanted to pay out Mr Pollock for something or another, so as Mr Pollock was looking at the view, with a telescrope, Mr Lloyd tied a little toy kitten on to 'the boy's' leg, soon Mr Pollock moved away and was surprised to find a rattling cat tied onto his leg? Mr Cunningham had had his revenge!

Tuesday

Today a troopship passed us looking very pretty, as she passed our band struck up but no reply was heard. Everyone at once said 'Ah! that settles it we're going to stay at Egypt' or 'Of course that means we're going on to the Cape!' (why it should nobody knows).

Wednesday

We got up at half past six, as we were supposed to arrive at Malta early in the morning. It was visible when we first came on deck and I could just Valette with my spectacles. At about 8 a.m. we entered the harbour. And passed two men-of-war (turret ships) Malta looked handsome from the sea, but still I think I'd rather [be] in Gib as they say Malta is not so nice inside. Presently crowds of little boats made their appearance and swarmed round the ship's side. The boats are called dissas, I don't know how spelt but pronounced like that. We did not go on shore it was delicous on deck with the sun pouring down on us. At 11.30 we started, our band played marches etc., and was answered by the band in one of the men of war, then we played Auld Lang Syne and finished up with Blue Bonnets over the Border as we steamed away from Malta. It really was delightful to see the hankerchiefs waving, to feel the sun blazing, and to hear the band playing. There was a slight swell after dinner which got worse towards tea time. Felt rather ill at tea went to sleep on deck afterwards, woke up feeling rather cold, Uncle Charlie got my coat and rapped me up with Pat in a shawl, who was feeling rather bad, he could not come down to dinner as he felt too ill. Came up on deck after dinner, feeling all right. Pat had recovered also.

Thursday

Much calmer today. It really is delicious on board – blue sea, blue sky. Nothing happened today worth notice.

Friday

Rather rougher today. I had a headache in the morning, which passed off afterwards. There was a violent squall during and after breakfast. Kept well during this day.

Saturday

We ought to be at Alexandria at about noon today. The sea had gone down a good deal during the night. A short time before luncheon we approached Alexandria the water was a *lovely* colour – an azure blue of the prettiest kind, and as we were gazing at it we saw a beautiful little boat with picturesque sails coming towards us, this was the pilot coming to show the way across the bar. The Himalaya stopped until the boat was alongside and when the pilot was on board she started again. Then we went down to luncheon during which we heard the most awful thumps imaginable – it was thought this was the ship going over the bar! After luncheon we found we were in the harbour safe and sound. In a short time we saw a steam launch approaching, it belonged to the Navy we could see, – ah! it must contain the orders concerning our embarkation etc! – great excitement! – the launch draws nearer – a swagger young lieutenant is visible with an eyeglass in his eye and – a large yellow envelope in his hand!! The launch is alongside – the young lieutenant is on deck – he is greeted with shouts of 'Hello Rosie how are you!' and 'Well Rosie my boy, glad to see you' and such like. Then followed shakings of hands. A pause in which the orders are given to the Colonel. Then the news is announced – the Black Watch is to proceed to Cairo at once, women and children to remain on board! It was reported that the Himalaya was sure to return to Malta. We were to start for Cairo tomorrow. The Grogans had a relation who was 1st Lieut. in the Undaunted a man of war in Alexandria, he came on board and invited the Grogans namely Major and Mrs Harvey and Aileen, and Aunt Aggie to tea on the Undaunted. Just as they were starting in the steam launch Major Grogan said Pat and I were to come too so we hopped in and were soon on board the Undaunted. Oh how clean and neat she looked compared with the Himalaya, everything was in perfect order. We then went below into the Captain's cabin and how cosy and comfortable it was – just like a little sitting room on land. Then one of the midshipmen showed Harvey, Grogan, Aileen, Pat and I over the ship, showed us the guns, from the twenty two pounder to the little baby one three feet long all of which you can move up and down with your little finger. Then we went into the gun-proof place in the mast, where there was also a gun. Then we went into the gun-room and had tea with the midshipmen – the whole thing was most entertaining. After tea we all returned to the Himalaya.

Sunday

There were two special trains to convey the troops to Cairo – one at nine a.m. the other at 10 a.m. We are to go in the second one. There was a great fuss all this morning getting the troops out (the heavy baggage had been taken out on Saturday). At last the first train started about a quarter of an hour late. There was a second class carriage for the officer's wives and children, the compartments all opening into one another. Uncle Charlie also came in our train but we only saw him at the station. A little before eleven our train started. Good-bye dear Himalaya! don't be to melancholy at the 42nd leaving you, because they *may* come back to you! One of the officers had telegraphed to George for some rooms in his hotel which luckily were not all engaged. George was the old messman of the 42nd and is greatly attached to them, he is now owner of the two best hotels in Cairo, viz Hotel Continental and Hotel d'Angleterre, which we are going to. It took about six hours to get to Cairo. The scenery en route was very curious. Perfectly flat country consisting of grass going on for ever, now and then a few date palms and camels. We stopped three times and each time we stopped, shouts of 'Verygoodoranges' (all in one word) were heard we tried to buy some and as we didn't know about the money we got cheated. We got a glimpse of the pyramids outside Cairo. When we arrived George (the hotel keeper) was there, and greeted us cordially. We then got into an omnibus and drove through Cairo, which I will shortly describe, to the Hotel D'Angleterre which is in a street branching off the main street.

Monday

Uncle Charle went to Abbassiyeh in the morning, where the 42nd are, it is three miles out of Cairo, in the desert. In the afternoon Uncle Charlie Aunt Aggie, Pat and I drove through Cairo. In the European quarter there are big houses, seperate from each other with gardens, palms grow in the streets which look just the same as each other, but in the Native town there are narrow streets crowded with Arabs in very picturesque blue dresses of different shades, sometimes a camel passes, laden with green green grass, it is a very pretty sight. There are bazaars with stalls in them on each side and you walk down and look at the things. Cairo is very pretty and picturesque.

Tuesday

In the afternoon Pat, Aileen and I rode on donkeys, it was great fun the donkeys flew and I greatly enjoyed myself. These donkeys would be priceless in England they hold their heads up and never think of stopping till they are told to and even then sometimes they won't. We went across the Nile to the polo ground and then back. The Nile is not blue but a sort of browny green.

Wednesday

Uncle Charlie, Aunt Aggie, Pat and I drove to Abbassiyeh and saw the desert a vast expanse of sand going on and on for ever. The barracks look very nice here.

Thursday

Meadows and Mrs Stuart's maid and Mrs Bramly's maid and Pat and I all started on donkeys for the Mosque at the citadel which is finest mosque in the world except that of Constanti-nople. We galloped off and soon got there, it is on a slight hill and overlooks Cairo. We had tickets of admittance and we had to put on big shoes over our boots. The first thing we saw was an alabaster court outside the mosque with fountain in the middle. Then we went into the mosque itself it is a square building with a low roof supported by alabaster pillars on the floor are the most exquisite carpets ever seen by man. There are two pulpits and lovely big glass chandeliers hang from the ceiling. We saw the old Khedive's clothes through a wire grating. They all sit on the floor and read the Koran, the Khedive included. It was a lovely place. Then we went into the court, where our donkey man opened a trap door and showed a well several hundred feet deep, then he opened another and there was a staircase which was supposed to go to Tunis. Then we got on donkeys and rode to Joseph's grave, a little way off. We got a guide who got a candle and went into a hole in a rock, we followed and went down and down a tunnel in the rock that went round and round and got deeper and deeper the guide went in front with the candle to light the way. The rock was cut strait down into a deep pit round which our tunnel descended. There were windows in it which gave a little light but not much. At last we reached the bottom and looking up you could see, hundreds of feet above you, up the pit. In an opening in the rock you could see two stones and between these Joseph is supposed to be buried. Then we saw Joseph's well and dropped stones down it. Then we toiled up to the level of the earth. Got on our donkeys again and rode off to the tombs of the Mamalukes, we had a delightful canter across the desert. We dismounted when we got there, put on the shoes and walked in. The tombs consist of three oblong blocks, one on the top of the other, getting smaller as they go up, they are beautiful. The tombs were made of alabaster and were all colours some were white with red and green ornamentations, some white and gold, but the best one of all was a black one with verses from the Koran written on in gold this was the largest, they were all lovely. Then we got on our donkeys and galloped back to the hotel.

Friday

Today the Comet was published. The Comet is a paper Pat and I wrote in the evenings. It was a great success. There was a double acrostic all in verse, two poems and several stories.

Saturday

Pat and I rode on donkeys to the Polo ground but nothing was going on so we came back.

Sunday

We go to the pyramids today as a good many people are able to come. A wagonet was ordered and the party consisted of Capt. and Mrs Campbell, Capt. and Mrs Bramley, Mr Maclaen, Capt. and Mrs Grant Pat and I, nine altogether. The pyramids are eight miles from Cairo the road is very pretty as there is an avenue of trees all the way, it is also very uneven and the carriage bumped up and down incessantly about half way we saw the pyramids vast and grand and towering above all things near them, they rose against the blue sky solemn and majestic. There is a hotel, a few minutes walk from the great pyramid, called Mena where we arrived at about 12.30. It was very hot and we sat in the verandah then we were asked if we would like to go over the hotel we said we would. It is the most beautiful hotel in the world it has, reading room, smoking room, breakfast room and drawing room all exquisitely furnished with old doors and screens and everything else imaginable. There is a lovely swimming bath in the open air, a chapel and a beautiful dining room the only disadvantage is that it is so far away from any town. While we had dinner a heavenly band played. After dinner we started for the pyramids, when we reached the base of the pyramid of Cheops we were surrounded by Arabs Uncle Charlie had already got a sheik who arranged matters. The idea is that you pay the sheik so much and he arranges for you going up the pyramid etc. Well, we were surrounded by Arabs and one seized each arm and hauled us up the pyramid. The steps are from three to four feet high.

My two Arabs helped me along very well and I rested two or three times during the ascent whenever I sat down they asked for backsheesh (tip) I said 'soon' so they said 'all right'. We went up on the shady side which was a good thing. I was fourth and it took a very short time to get up I should think I did it in about ten minutes. I forgot to say that several subalterns joined the party at Mena. The view from the top was extraordinary, one could see the desert, a mass of sand stretching on and on as far as the eye could reach and one could see the green grass fields where the desert ended and where cultivation began and one could see the long straight road going to Cairo and everything perfectly flat all round, Cairo in the distance and the blue sky overhead. Coming down was easier than going I thought but other people didn't. I simply jumped from step to step the Arabs holding my hands. Before coming down we saw two men race to the top of the other pyramid which is very difficult to get up because there are no steps at the top and it is glazed over. One of the men went down our pyramid and up the other in under ten minutes! He looked a speck on the other pyramid an ant on an ant hill! When we reached the bottom it was settled that we would not go inside as it is so very stuffy and dirty. Aunt Aggie said she thought it would be a good idea to go to the sphinx on camels, directly she mentioned this word fifteen camels were on us, all making the most awful noise when sitting down. We were all seized by at least four men who pulled us in four different directions I got to a Camel and an Arab said it was a lady's one, which it was not so I was hussled off and two men came and lifted me into the air and put [me] on a camel at this moment the sheik interfered and I got onto the one that was supposed to have had a lady's saddle. It was rather a ghastly sensation when the camel got up and you thought you were going to tumble off. We walked on our camels to the sphinx where we dismounted and walked to a place just opposite its face. Although its nose had entirely gone it looked as if all its features were there. What an exquisite face is it – how solemn – how majestic you look, your eyes looking out into the desert with that beautiful expression always on your face so collosal and so perfect. You, who have been there for thousands and thousands of years, you, who have gazed and gazed at that endless sea of sand ever since you existed, tell me oh tell me how to look with that sublime expression on your face at all that comes and all that goes, careless of everything for ever. What a lovely picture it was the camels in the foreground and at the back the Sphinx, the diety of all that's peaceful and of all that's grand. The pyramids too, were visible the one of Cheops on the right and the smaller ones on the left. We then walked to the temple of the Sphinx, which had been dug up from under the sand, there were great pieces of granite about sixteen feet high and about four feet square. They were not polished but cut exactly square and correct, there was a lot of the granite lying about. We got on the camels and half of the party went to a place called Campbell's well and the other half consisting of Uncle Charlie, Aunt Aggie and I went back to give another look at the beloved Sphinx, sad I was to leave her, but I felt sure that she was happy and ever would be. Of course I was pestered for backsheesh by the camel boy all the way. We had tea in the verandah of the hotel, while the band played sweetly. After tea we drove home in the middle one of our horses kicked over the trace, upon which the coachman violently whipped him to make him jump back again, which of course he could not go, however Capt. Campbell got out and undid the trace, which let the horse get into his right position. We got to d'Angleterre without further incident. Mr Dick Cunningham had been called a wild gazelle by the Arabs, which is amusing, he being the fattest of the fat.

Tuesday

This is Shrove Tuesday and the Carnival begins at 2.0 p.m. We had settled to go to the Egyptian Museum at Giseh today, which has all the mummies in it, however Major Grogan had gone there in the morning and found that it shut up in the afternoon because of the carnival, so we couldn't go, but instead we got seats in the Continental stand to see the carnival procession pass. Mr & Mrs Maclean and Mrs Campbell came as well. We bought some confetti and a shovel and pelted the people violently. The streets were crammed and at first nothing particular happened. Soon the grand procession came. First of all there was a long string of horses two and two with postillions on their backs these (the horses) dragged a large sort of caravan with lots of men in it the men were masked. When the caravan got nearly opposite us, there was a block in the road and it stopped, the men inside showered confetti upon us, and I should think it *did* hurt, you saw the horrid shovel aimed straight at you and then whiz, through the air came the confetti all over you and around you. In vain, you returned the volley but alas their masks sheilded them and they cared not! At last the caravan went on, and the next thing was very pretty. It was a procession of camels very sweetly got up with the same kind of thing as is draped above the drawing room door, only red. On their backs were men, some with tom-toms and some with little sort of pipes. Then came a sedan chair supported by camels and then a camel with a palm stuck into its saddle. This takes place whenever there is a wedding in the sedan chair sits the bride. Then there were a lot of other caravans and different things not very interesting. There was one rather pretty thing and that was a carriage powdered all over the people inside were powdered the coachman was powdered *and* the horses were too, there was a person in it dressed in pink which gave a little bit of colour to it. There was also a vast pyramid with people on it but it did not pass our stand. It was very amusing was the carnival and I enjoyed it immensly.

Thursday

Aunt Aggie, Meadows, Pat and I went to the museum this afternoon. It is a little way across the Nile. It used to be a palace belonging to a pasha and it has lovely large rooms and very nice gardens. We saw the hyroglyphs of the Egyptians and lovely old statues of Egyptians men and women and we saw the piece of stone on which was written a statement showing that the sphinx was standing when the pyramids were being built, we also saw the jewels of an Egyptian queen – the most lovely things I ever saw. After wandering through several rooms we came to the great hall where the mummies are. There on each side of you are the kings that held almighty sway in the country, then so powerful, in which they were ruling. Realise their greatness by the relics that they left behind them – the giant pyramids which towering above all men, rise in splendour and magnificence and more wonderful still that sublime diety, whom men call the sphinx, who look forever into endless time! These monarchs lie around you – what an extraordinary thing! The best known by us is Rameses II, the pharoah of Moses, he has the most curious face imagineable, his nose large and the lower part of his face small in proportion, but all is hideous and capable of the utmost tyranny. It is a weird sight in the dim light of the room to see the face of Pharoah, the face of the man who forms one of the most principle features in the beginning of the Bible, a ghastly spectacle all black from age is that ancient ruler of Egypt. He had a little tiny curl of hair on his head. We also saw his father and grandfather and a high priest, whose nails were quite perfect and showed he must have used nail scissors! We saw as well a princess and her baby, they were both wrapped up so you could not see their faces. We then went into a place where there were little antiquities to be bought, as these were kept by the museum they were sure to be real so I got a little god made of blue stone, he is very sweet and comes from a tomb. Aunt Aggie has got a lovely big one. How interesting it all has been – How glad I am I came to Egypt and saw all these wondrous sights.

Sunday

We went to rather a nice little church in the morning, the singing was good.

Tuesday

Aunt Aggie, Meadows, Harry, Pat and I went on donkeys to the bazaars we rode through them, it was great fun, several of them are built round some old mosque with lovely musharabiyeh windows and sweet arches. It's very pretty looking down a street at the end of which is a stately mosque with high minarets ascending into the blue sky the streets are traversed by men and women the former clothed in a lovely blue raiment, the latter enveloped in black.

Saturday 27th

We're woken up by Meadows who said that the Himalaya started on Sunday and so we had to pack up with all speed as the train started at 9.30 a.m. Aunt Aggie and Uncle Charlie would join us at Suez with the regiment. Mrs Grogan and her kids and Capt. and Mrs Bramly were going in our train to Alexandria and Harry Grogan too. So off we drove from Angleterre at nine o'clock arrived at the station in time (for a wonder) and were soon puffing away from beloved Cairo. It really was a delightful place, the donkey rides, the bazaars and the pyramids are only to be found at Cairo. Little did I expect it to be like it was, the hot sunshiny days and the sitting out on the hotel porch were so enjoyable and now good-bye to all this, once more am I to toss on the ocean for a few weeks and see more wonders and more foreign lands. The journey to Alexandria was loathsome. The dust was appalling in ten minutes there was a thick layer of it on our boxes, our clothes, our faces, our hats, our everything! It was actually worse than London! We had to sponge our faces when we got to Alexandria. There was a good deal of bother getting our luggage and ourselves into a cab, but at last this difficulty was got over and we drove for the docks. Alexandria is a dull town with nothing worthy of note in it. We were on board the Himalaya again at half past two (p.m.)

Sunday 28th

Mrs Grogan, Aileen, Pat and I went to church on the 'Undaunted' it was a very nice service. I forgot to say that we came here to tea yesterday. Of course the ship didn't start today.

Monday 29th

Departed from Alexandria at 4 p.m. today. We had the ship all to ourselves, which was a blessing.

Tuesday 30th

Arrived at Port Said at 8 a.m. It consisted of several houses on the brink of the desert by the water's edge, there were several large breakwaters there. We stayed here for two hours. We then entered the canal. It is extraordinary, on each side stretches the desert and behind you is the Suez Canal long and thin and straight. At first there was a lake on each side, it was then we saw a mirage. Beyond the lake there was sand as far as the eye could reach just on the horizon. One could see water and the hills of sand came out of it like islands, really there was no water there at all it was the reflection of the lake. We were very lucky to have seen this as I believe it is very rare. In the night we tied up and in doing this got stuck right across the canal. This was a great bore, but at last we managed to get free. Several ships passed us with beautiful electric lights in their bows they were so strong one couldn't look at them.

Wednesday 1st Mar

My birthday today – how odd – a birthday in the Suez Canal! Got to Ismalia at 7 a.m. this morning. We go at an average of 5 knots an hour sometimes we go 8 and the waves we make nearly breaks the canal's side down. It is narrower today. Every now and then we pass a little red brick house with a brown roof and green trees growing round it, they look so pretty. At 4 p.m. we arrived at Suez a wee town on the edge of the desert. We couldn't have the birthday cake today as it was not iced. A letter from Aunt Aggie saying she would see us at four on Friday.

Thursday 2nd

The Padre said he would take Pat and I ashore to see the cricket match if we liked, of course we did, and went off in the steam cutter to the shore. The match was between the Himalaya and Suez, Suez won easily. Pat and I picked up some exquisite shells. We rode to the cricket ground on donkeys we also rode back. It was very nice having a day on shore. The Padre was very kind.

Friday 3rd

Madam Grant came on board at the stroke of four, the regiment to follow tomorrow morning. We then ate the birthday cake which was not very good.

Saturday 4th

42nd embarked at 8 in the morning. We started from Suez at 10 a.m.

Sunday

In the gulf of Suez all day.

Monday 6th

The Red Sea. Temperature about 80.

Tuesday

It was so hot in Pandemonium tonight we had to get out of bed and go and sleep in the saloon!

Wednesday 8th

The band played 'The barren rocks of Aden' as we steamed into the harbour we went very close to some rocks which were a very pretty red colour. Aden itself looks like an island from the sea, and very barren. Directly we weighed anchor lots of little boats came out from the shore with little black boys in them all shouting 'Have a dive sir? Have a dive' 'Ohoa Ohoa Have a dive sir, have a dive' 'Ohoa! Ohoa!' clapping their hands. We threw in sixpences and they dived down and brought up the sixpences in their mouths, they swam exquisitely and were quite at home in the water as in their boats. All the afternoon we were coaling and the coal dust poured down on us like rain by tea time our face and hands were literally black. Aunt Aggie and Uncle Charlie had dinner on the shore tonight at the hotel. It was terribly hot all day.

Thursday 9th

We meant to have breakfast on shore in the hotel but Uncle Charlie's lateness made us miss the first boat and we didn't start till ten o'clock. The people in our boat were Capt. Rose, Captain and Mrs Stuart and maid, Capt. and Mrs Grant and two sons and maid. When on shore we walked to the hotel where Capt. and Mrs Stuart and their maid and Meadows separated from us we had breakfast in the hotel. The great thing in Aden are the tanks, which are very old and very large, they are on the other side of the town. After breakfast we drove out to there, Uncle Charlie and Capt. Rose in one cab, Aunt Aggie, Pat and I in another. The town is surrounded by rocky hills which are volcanic the town being in the crater. It is half Indian, half Egyptian the view down the streets making pretty pictures with the grey rock in the background and the quaint little houses on each side. The people wear very nice clothes richly coloured. We went through the camel market crowded with camels in different attitudes. When we got to the tanks we got out and walked round the largest, it holds 4,000,000 gallons when full, and is simply enormous there is nothing in it as there has not been rain here for 2 years! It was boiling! We drove back and Aunt Aggie made some purchases in the town. From the hotel we walked to the club where we had some lemon squash. From the club's verandah you can see the sea, and as we were looking over, a naval officer, who was with us, saw an octopus in the water, we went down to the water's edge and buzzed stones at it to make it move and it became the same colour as every stone it sat on. The naval officer said he would give to a little boy who was there a rupee if he got it, so the little boy jumped into the water but unfortunately frightened the beast away. Shortly after we were taken in the steam cutter to the Himalaya, at six she started for Mauritius. I forgot to say yesterday that as we were sitting on deck someone said 'Here comes a P & O' we looked and saw – 'The Coromandel' and sure enough it was the old Coromandel!

Friday 10th

It was slightly cooler today though of course still very hot. It is simply terrible in pandemonium the air is poisonous but we are hardly ever down there as we sleep in the saloon.

Saturday 11th

Hotter today, this heat is worse than the Red Sea heat as it is damp and sticky, in the Red Sea it is a dry heat.

Sunday 12th

Usual service in the morning.
Aden was not such a bad place on the whole, of course it was very hot but it was a dry heat and not very disagreeable. Troops coming home from India are always quartered here for a year. The scenery is fine, and bold and the rugged rock, which everywhere meets your eye is magnificent.

March 22nd

Got to Mauritius early this morning. It was so nice to see something green again. We went ashore for luncheon. The first thing we did after we landed was to buy some pugaries for our hats as the sun was so strong. It really was terribly hot, however I didn't mind it much. After luncheon we went to Curepipe by train. Curepipe is up in the hills. In the train we had a very good view of the country. The hills were most extraordinary they looked as if they were going to fall down every minute, they were not at all grand, but looked drunk and misshapen. When we got to Curepipe it was raining we drove to the hotel, where we were going to stay the night. It continued raining all day. The air was horrid and one could not help feeling depressed.

23rd

Last night we slept in an outhouse, I mean a little house with four bedrooms in it. We woke up, it was raining again – it always rains in this place – we rushed over to the hotel for breakfast, after breakfast we hastened to the station, got into a train and steamed off for Port Louis. We got out at that place and were soon on board the Himalaya again. Aunt Aggie and Uncle Charlie then rowed back to shore to see the Mauritius half of the regiment off. I was so sorry at parting with so many old friends. The 64th (the regiment quartered in Mauritius before) all looked yellow (Mauritius is a very bad place for fever). We departed from this loathsome isle at 4 o'clock. Really it is a horrid place, so boiling in Port Louis, so rainy and so damp in the hills, where the regiment is quartered.

24th Thursday

Squall today and a very good thing too after the hot weather, as it clears it all away and freshens us up a bit.

25th Mar

Much cooler today.

April 1st

Entered Table Bay at half past six this morning. Table Mountain looks exquisite and just what I expected it to be like. There is a good deal of green about the base of it. It was so hot in the middle of the day that I had to go down into the saloon.

Table Mountain and Cape Town

April 2nd

Easter Sunday today. Sunday is truly a terrible day on board ship, you can't do anything.

April 3rd

Aunt Aggie went ashore looking for houses she found a very nice little one at Mowbray (a suburb of Cape Town). Luckily Uncle Charlie had lodging allowance (£50 a year).

Tuesday April 4th

The troops disembark as soon as the ship gets into dock but at present there is no room, but as a ship goes out tomorrow we will be able to go in. Pat and I have not been ashore yet. Looking back I see I have not said why we did not go to Natal after Mauritius. The reason was that there was smallpox at Mauritius (as there always is) and so after going to Mauritius we would have twenty one days quarantine, which would not be sweet, but at Cape Town the Governor has the right of abolishing quarantine, which is neat. So they are going to Natal on the way back.

Wednesday 5th

General Cameron came on board this afternoon greatly to the captain's annoyance because he wanted to get into dock as soon as possible. The general came to 'Inspect the guards' N.B. He has no more right to inspect the guards than I have! He talks very slowly and said 'I am making quite an informal visit and I won't keep you long as I am going to the "Leipsig" ' 'So am I' says the captain 'I'll take you in my boat if you like'. The 'Leipsig' is a German man of war on which there is a dance today. The general was introduced to the 42nd officers. He stayed on board for about twenty minutes. At five we started for the dock, it was very difficult to get in as we had to go round very sharp corners, at the end the ship was pulled right round by the men. We were all right at 6.30.

Thursday 6th

Got up at 6 a.m. this morning to see the regiment disembark, and had to wait half an hour. The Cape Highlanders (volunteers) played the pipes as they were marching away. They did look so lovely especially after their sea kit which consists of blue trousers and coats and Neapolitan fisherman's hats, only blue. As they marched off there seemed a great many of them, although there was only half a regiment. The Cape Highlanders think themselves far superior to the Black Watch!!! After breakfast Arthur Marindin took Pat and I to the station where we met Aunt Aggie and Meadows. Then we went into Cape Town to make some purchases. It is a most magnificent place with palacial buildings and shops worthy of Bond Street but it is very small, everything is next door to everything else.

Thursday 6th April

After we had finished shopping we returned to the station where we met Uncle Charlie we then had luncheon, after which we went in the train for Wynberg, Uncle Charlie stayed behind. It was pretty in the train, Table Mountain looked so grand, and the pines and blue-gums looked so lovely. All the villages between Wynberg and Cape Town are not exactly suburbs (in the London sense) but are quite in the country though they are only from three to eight miles off the Metropolis. Wynberg is the most well known because the camp is there. We arrived at this place at about 1.30. The soil is *bright* terra cotta, and the roads are all beautiful avenues of pines or blue-gums and oaks. Cogill's Hotel is quite close to the station however we drove to it in a Cape-cart as there were bags and things. A Cape-cart is a delightful vehicle drawn by two horses on two wheels it has a hood and the people don't sit back to back as in a dog-cart but all four facing the front. Arrived at Cogill's we had luncheon (the other being only lunch). In the afternoon we went to look at a house close by it was very small and dark and not at all nice.

ADDENDA OF DIARY

I'm now going to write down all the things that I have forgotten to put down in their proper places. Dorothy may be interested to hear that I saw the hag (of s.s. Coromandel) in Cairo! Every second day there was fire drill which was rather amusing sometimes the fire was supposed to be in the bows, sometimes midships sometimes in the stern they had great squirts and they squirted the water into the sea. All the skylights were shut and the sailors scurried about all over the deck. Once they had 'Man overboard' a buoy was dropped which burnt in the water, so as they should see it in the night, the ship was stopped and as quick as lightning a boat was lowered which at once rowed for the buoy, in five minutes they had reached it and had it on board and in another five minutes they were back on ship! They did it very smartly. Of course, jokes at once began – 'It's not a man overboard but a boy' and such like. Every night at mess after the wine had been round, the president tapped on the table and said 'The queen' – 'The queen' 'The queen' 'The queen' echoed down the lines and then from above was heard 'God save the queen' played by the band. I was so sorry to leave the Himalaya, and I still am. She is the greatest roller in the navy (quite true). And yet (excuse the boast) I was never sick all the time I was on her! Mine is indeed a unique experience – a peep behind the scenes, in the midst of a regiment for five weeks, knowing them all and liking them all, except – ah I must not say.

We had a sail-bath every morning after the Red Sea. It

consisted of two baths made of sails on the deck, it went on from 6 to 7.30 a.m. of course it was sea water only quite warm. The baths were filled by hose, one for each bath, and the great thing was to turn your hose on the wretch in the next bath, then he squirted back at you, then there was a great fight, accompanied by yells from everyone, especially from those whose pyjamas were being doused with water. It was great fun. Pat and I hopped in whenever anyone hopped out and then when we were turned out by someone waiting to go in, we waited till he got out and then we hopped in again! We lived in the sail-bath. Hence we were christened 'The Water Babies'! Everyone looked forward to the sail-bath – it was the great event of the day. Every day there were at least three fights once Pat and I were sent in and were squirted by both the creatures at the same time! (which was a swindle) Very often when we won a fight our bath was invaded by the defeated one and we either had to fly or our heads were held under water till we begged for mercy! (which was also a swindle)!

On the first day after leaving Suez all the sailors put on their white coats and I put on my thin things. It got very hot in the Red Sea we had to desert our pandemonium bunks and go into the saloon to sleep. The Red Sea was not very disagreeable in heat as it was dry and not damp. But the worst time was between the line and Mauritius it was so wet, damp and hot you felt as if you could not do a thing and your clothes stuck to you, and your face perspired all the day. It was pretty bad from Aden to the line, but after the line it was much worse as there was a head wind so we got no breeze, and one of the awnings was taken off to make us go quicker. Luckily it got much cooler after Mauritius, which was a great relief but in Table Bay it was terribly hot, the people in Cape Town said those were the hottest days they had had all summer. I enjoyed the voyage very much indeed it was so entertaining and interesting – oh! it is like some beautiful dream.

Friday 7th April 1893

Cogill's Hotel is not very comfortable and *very* expensive. The walks here are lovely, every road is an exquisite avenue of beautiful trees with the red, red earth below, and the sky and the mountain above. It seems so quiet here after the ship!

Saturday 8th

Meadows, Pat and I went to the camp, it is quite close to the hotel and made a very nice little walk. The air there is lovely, and you get a splendid view of the veldt and the mountains beyond. The camp is very nice and is not at all damp like the rest of Wynberg. The barrack rooms are one behind the other going up the hill, they look very clean inside. We glanced into the messwindows and it looked beautiful!

Sunday 9th April

Pat and I were so terribly bitten by animals in the night that we could hardly sleep at all. We went to morning service, very pretty church, good singing, sermon terrible!

Monday 10th

Uncle Charlie has engaged the Mowbray House, and a good thing too! The McLean's house is one minute's walk from ours which is so nice. We have got it for four months (perhaps longer).

Tuesday 11th

Aunt Aggie has found a boarding house in Mowbray where we are going to stay till we get into our own house, as the hotel is so expensive. Wynberg gets very damp in the wet weather and is a very bad place for throats so it is a good thing we are going to live in Mowbray. I forgot to say on Monday, Aunt Aggie and the rest of us went to see the camp again, and we all wished that the 42nd was there instead of the 15th.

Wednesday 12th

At 12 o'clock we departed from the wretched Gogill's and drove off for Mowbray in a Cape cart, the luggage went by train with Taylor. The drive was delightful and rather jolty. Of course it is quite in the country and very pretty. Wynberg is about five miles from Mowbray and eight from Cape Town, so everything is very close to everything. We got to the boarding house (Charlton House) just in time for luncheon, we sleep in a house next door belonging to two very nice old ladies, the Misses McLear, daughters of Sir John Maclear, the boarding house belongs to Mrs Bright, her history is that she was the wife of a governor of a province up country, he suddenly died, leaving her destitute, so she determined to set up a boarding house – and did. She is quite a lady. I shall never forget that luncheon, it was too funny. Mrs Bright asked everyone which they would have. The food was very good. Pat and I played croquet in the Maclear's garden.

Tuesday 18th

Lieut. Plumber of the Himalaya is now stationed in Simon's Town (about an hour and a half's train from Cape Town) and he invited Pat and I to go up and have a day's fishing with him today. I think partly because at every port, coming out, we fished – and not one fish did we catch! and partly because Simon's Town is an *excellent* place for fishing. It was very kind of him to ask us to go there. We went off in the train after breakfast and got to Simon's Town at about 12. The train winds in and out quite close to the sea between Wynberg and Simon's Town, the view is lovely the mountain on one side, and the sea so blue, and the mountains behind it on the other. The sea-smell was most refreshing but what was not quite so nice was the stiff South Easter that was blowing. At Simon's Town Station we were met by Mr Plumber who said that it was too windy to go out fishing and that if we tried we would get drenched! He gave us an excellent dinner at the club and then took us to see a torpedo boat (in dock). She was wee, one could only just get into the Captain's Cabin and instead of a companion way there was a ladder. Then we went on board H.M.S. Swallow, she is a nice little boat. On board we met a delightful little fat man, he showed up over the ship and made jokes of the most absurd nature, there was also another man who gave us some sweet little figures and a bit of native African money, which is most curious, made of iron and in this shape.

We then rowed off to the 'Penelope' Mr Plumber's ship, I had quite a shock when I went on board, she was so clean and white. Mr Plumber showed us all over her which was most interesting, we saw the most fascinating guns in the world and worked them all! Then we had tea in Mr Plumber's cabin, which was beautiful. We got rather wet going ashore where we had a game of billiards (at the club) and did not cut the cloth! We then proceeded to the railway station and it was quite dark when we got home. Mr Plumber was very kind.

Wednesday 19th April

Hooray! today we move into our house I am most excited to see what the inside is like, the outside is sweet, it has two stories and a double verandah (which none of the other Mowbray houses have) and a very pretty creeper with a white and red flower growing up it, there is a little bit of garden in front (disgracefully kept) with a Norfolk pine in the middle, behind there is a fowl run and some uncultivated land, the name is Delgany. We carried all the light things over from the boarding house as it is only two minutes walk, the heavy things were taken over in a cart. The drawing room is pretty big, it has terra-cotta walls and was filled with ghastly objects – filthy little brackets – disgusting grasses – appalling vases and shells! the walls are covered with terrible pictures! We counted the chairs and found that there were 16! 2 sofas! and 1 music-stool! The

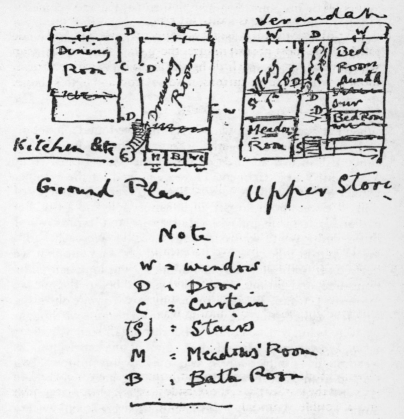

dining-room is not too bad, and the sitting room upstairs is filled with very nice books.

I was to go to England by the Trojan, a Union Boat, which left Cape Town on Wed. 10th May. Aunt Aggie made desperate efforts to find someone who was going in that boat, but she met with no success. This was rather sad. I wanted very much to go home in the Trojan because it stopped at St Helena, The Canary Islands and Madiera, places which I wanted to see. Aunt Aggie and I used often to go out driving together (in a Cape cart) to pay calls; and Pat, who was not at all interested in the extraordinary inhabitants of Cape Town, went out for long rides on his pony 'Tommy'. Sometimes Pat and I climed a little way up Table Mountain, which was beautiful. Once we went up to an old house called the Block House, which used to belong to the Dutch, who used [it] for keeping off the Natives. There are some canon on a platform in front of it.

Friday 12th May

When Pat and I came down to breakfast we found a letter on each of our plates! Eagerly opening them we found they contained an invitation to dinner at the Mess from Arthur Marindin! Vast excitement! How we longed for the evening. Dinner was at 8, and I'm sure we began to get ready in plenty of time. We were both dressed in our most splendid attire. Pat had on his dress kilt and white sporran etc. and I wore my best Etons and a white waistcoat and black tie. We each had a lovely button hole. We were so afraid of being late that we hurried off to the station (one minute's walk) long before the right time, and got into a train that started before the one we meant to get into. In consequence of this we were shivering with fright all the time we were in the train because we thought we were being whisked off to Johannisburg or somewhere far away. However we arrived after hours of anxious waiting as we thought – only really it was only twenty minutes! We walked from Cape Town station to the barracks, which were close by, and went into the anteroom. We had to march into dinner first. By Aunt Aggie's injunction we were not allowed to have any alcoholic drinks accept to drink the queen's health, so I had lemon squash. I sat next to Arthur Marindin and Pat on the other side of him. After dinner, when the wine had been passed round, Capt. Gordon who was the mess president rose and said 'Mr Vice – The queen'. Then Mr Dick Cunningham said 'Gentlemen The Queen', then we all stood up and drank the queen's health! After some time I saw Capt. Gordon making a sign to the others and they all got up, we did not know in the least what was happening were going to follow their example, when they told us to sit down. Capt. Gordon then said 'I beg to propose the health of the Rt. Hon. Prime

Minister Lytton Strachey and Field Marshal Sir Patrick Grant! Hear, hear was heard from several voices – soon afterwards we went into the anteroom. Then I left my card on the mess. After that we had a game of whist with Capt. Gordon and Arthur Marindin, which was most amusing – Arthur and I won. Then it was discovered that it was very late and that if we did not hurry we should miss our train; so we hastily put on our coats and dashed out, Arthur Marindin accompanying us. As we left we were cheered by the officers! We ran with all speed to the station, my tie streaming in the breeze! We got there in plenty of time and were soon steaming off to Mowbray.

4

AFTER TWO DISASTROUS *terms at Abbotsholme, an experimental 'New School', Strachey was transferred in the summer of 1894 to a 'semi-demi public school' at Leamington. His painful awkwardness and odd spindly appearance were at once seized upon by the other boys who nicknamed him 'Scraggs' and singled him out for bullying. 'At school I used to weep — oh! for very definite things,' he later confided to Leonard Woolf, '—bitter unkindness and vile brutality.' But after the first year this bullying abated, and he seems to have settled down comfortably. By 1896 he was a school prefect, head of his house, and fairly bored.*

It was at Leamington that Strachey experienced his first homosexual crushes. They stirred in him emotions so violent that later on he came to see them as symbolizing the ideal companionship which he was always seeking to recapture in adult life. While still in his first year, he conceived a dumb idyllic devotion for one of the older boys who, by partly eradicating Strachey's self-consciousness, induced in him a state of ecstatic self-oblivion. Magically he felt himself released from the prison of his own hateful physique. This was his first real passion, and it involved what he always considered to be his purest feelings — 'that good kind of exquisite abolition of oneself in such a heaven-born hero', as he described it to Leonard Woolf. '. . . Part of, don't you think, came from what we certainly can never get again — that extraordinary sense of corporal hugeness of our God? To be able to melt into a body literally twice as big as one's own.'

The following pages of his diary, its theme half-concealed under a facetious title and with occasional bursts of hiero-glyphics, records 'the second of my desperate businesses at school'. His choice of hero, as on the first occasion, was someone very dissimilar to himself – a dashing young batsman and footballer named George Underwood, very freckled and athletic and with red hair that dazzled Strachey. These two infatuations formed the pattern of much of his adult love-life, and, as he explains in his last diary 'A Fortnight In France', he was particularly reminded of his feelings for George Under-wood thirty years later when in love with Roger Senhouse.

THE STORY OF SIR JOHN SNOOKS, KT, WRITTEN BY HIMSELF IN THE REIGN OF OUR SOVEREIGN QUEEN ELIZABETH AND IN THE YEAR OF OUR LORD 1586

At the University of Cambridge
Summer Term

NOV. 13th 1896. Friday

It has long been in my mind to write down every day my thoughts and deeds as they come to me; and now as I sit alone in my study, the window open to let in the cool air, the darkness covering all things I will begin.

I cannot remember when I first began to think of * as I do now: in fact I think there was always in my mind the seed from which my present thoughts have sprung. But it was this term that the tree first began to blossom, to bear fruit. A year ago he came here and even then I †ed him, – and his ‡'s. But now I know more of him, & I converse with him, I feel with him in a more developed and substantial way. This term I began afresh and have I think not wasted my time. I have seen him open his eyes and stare (mentally) at me, I have seen his mind gradually grasping me, he has come to me more often, he has thought about me more and more, and now – what? Is there any hope of his ever †ing me? It began, this later development in a way by accident; he came into my study (I think to try and find out what sort of a person I was) – and asked some trivial question. And then I began to talk to him, and at last reached his mind a little through – indecency. Measure for measure, Venus and Adonis, Lucrece (I remember his curious pronunciation). We

85

came through this to other things – we touched lightly the very foundations almost; but lightly, and then he went, leaving me with a heart leaping with excitement. And this very excitement proves, I think that my † for him was no recent acquirement so to speak. I suppose the result of the interview was not altogether unsatisfactory to him. He came again, and began to get more and more intimate. How well I remember the Sunday walk, the way, the joy, the converse. The quaintness of his manner, his charm, his piquancy! And the strain running through the whole tenor of his words like the refrain in a quaint old sonata – to burst forth with all the rush and vigour of a thousand instruments in one wild cataract of glory. This to my *mind*. It was the confession that he †ed some one with all his might. And I told him the same. Ah God! it was happy! and so long ago! So we grew more friendly by degrees, till at last one afternoon, three days ago, the confession was on my lips. He mentioned † – the † of women. I said, thinking of the † greater than that of women 'You know who Jonathan was, he—' then who should come in but Providence in the shape of Tommy Clarke[1] to put an end to everything. And running parallel with my thoughts on * have been my thoughts on Plato. This term I read for the first time, with a rush of mingled pleasure and pain the Symposium 'the story of the feast: and Agathon and Diotima seemed from death and dark forgetfulness released' as great Shelley says. That day of surprise, relief, and fear to know that what I feel now was felt 2000 years ago in glorious Greece. Would I have lived then, would I had sat at the feet of Socrates, seen Alcibiades, wondrous Alcidiades, Alcibiades, the abused, but the great, felt with them all, †ed with them all! How can I describe my young †? Shall I compare him to a summer's day? (I may be sinning, but I am doing so in the company of Shakespeare and Greece.) His hair is a bright beautiful copper, his complexion grand, expression grand, lips grand, his eyes are unfortunately wrong they should be black, they are a sort of green, which is distressing: his ‡'s—! Impossible to describe, marvellous in beauty, fulness, sensa-

[1] This was probably 'Ruffus' Clarke. See page 179.

tion, colour. And now I am waiting for him to come, will he? I must walk down the passage, into the prep-room – anywhere – I *must* get him.

Sunday Nov. 29th

I find it impossible to keep this diary as regularly as I could have wished; so I must content myself with putting down from time to time my thoughts, and acts: the latter not so much, as they are comparatively unimportant. Since I last wrote the * affair has been progressing as usual. I think of late he has been taking less interest in me – we have had no philosophical conversations for a long time – and I have certainly often found myself asking whether it is worth while keeping up this thing – whether his ignorance, uncultivatedness, and his general nonchalance do not overbalance his magnetic charm, and his beauty. His beauty too; – is he so beautiful? At times no; but *always* yes! He has just been with me, and I am continually trying to take the final plunge and declare my † for him. What would he do? What would he do? I know his † is given to another, not apparently to §, ‖. or ¶. – could it be to George or possibly ʃ? Scandal says to ¶. I cannot make it out.

Monday Nov. 30th

Was introduced by the entrance of Clarke looking, as usual, for *, not finding him, he suggested that I should go out with him. I agreed. Shortly after * came in and after a lot of ragging, painful for me to witness, they went out together. Soon however, Clarke came back, as he thought it was too cold: imagine leaving * because of the cold! That's just the maddening part; these people continually enjoy * company, and never seem to care, while I am thankful if I have 5 mins. with him.

This is the list for Sunday.
1. A[fter] B[reakfast]
2.   „   „
3. B[efore] C[hapel]

4. B[efore] D[inner]
5. A[fter] D[inner]
6.   „   „
7.   „   „
8. B[efore] T[ea]
9. A[fter] T[ea]
10. A[fter] S[upper]

10 times in all. A record I think. At No. 8 he told me my †
was Farmer! I laughed and gave him no denial, at No. 9 he also
hinted at it, and I am disposed to let him think so. No. 10 was
the best. When the gas was out he lay on the chair and said he
was going to sleep there. I saw my opportunity, tucked the
[word illegible] round him, said 'good-night master Georgie!
and /ed him! It was a never-to-be-forgotten moment. The
shortest in the world. The outward forms /ed, did our souls?
No no, a thousand times, never will that happen I am afraid.
And how petty this place is without †! Indeed I don't know
what I should have done this term if it had not been for the
excitement of *. Exciting it is indeed, how exciting few know.
Certainly Gaitskell[2] doesn't, who is sitting in his chair at this
moment, reading Pearson's Monthly.

[2] Gaitskell was one of the school prefects and 'quite a fool'.

5

STRACHEY WAS ONLY *seventeen when he left Leamington, too young, his mother judged, to go straight up to Oxford or Cambridge. Fortunately the family had a special connection with Liverpool University College (as it then was) through Lytton's cousin Sir Charles Strachey, who had married Ada Raleigh, sister of that most spirited of dons, Walter Raleigh. Raleigh was at this time King Alfred Professor of English Literature at Liverpool, and it was here that Strachey went in October 1897.*

During his two years at Liverpool he lodged at 80 Rodney Street – just across the road from where Gladstone had been born. It was a sombre, dignified street of Georgian houses, full of sombre, dignified professional men and their middle-class families. Typical of the inhabitants were Strachey's landlords Dr and Mrs Alexander Stookes, whom he nicknamed 'Spookes'. At first they had been apprehensive of having a young student in the house, fearing that he would be rowdy and irresponsible. But Strachey turned out to be a model lodger, quiet, unobtrusive and invariably polite in suffering himself to be introduced to all their friends, the medical fraternity of Liverpool. Their relief was manifest. 'The boy has proved a delightful companion and no trouble to either of us,' Dr Stookes wrote to Lady Strachey after Lytton's first term. 'We could hardly have imagined that it would have been possible to have a stranger guest with so little friction.'

As this diary shows, Strachey's time at Liverpool was incomparably dreary, without love or success of any kind. His best moments were spent in exploring second-hand bookshops and going for prodigious bicycle rides as far away as possible from Liverpool.

Nearly thirty years later Strachey was offered the Chair of English Literature at Liverpool University but refused it.

DIARY 1898

March 3rd

Many times before have I got a book and written in it my thoughts and my actions. But my previous attempts have always been crowned with failure: — inasmuchas after 2, 3 or possibly 4 entries the diary came to an end. Another effort! God knows there is small enough reason for it. My other autobiographical writings were the outcome of excitements really quite out of the commonplace: but this is *begun*, at any rate, in the veriest dog days imaginable.

The chief interest in a diary consists in the rereading of it long after the events recorded have taken place, and when the feelings and thoughts resulting therefrom are dim and faint in the memory. My great-Aunt Eliza[1] must have been a wonderful woman to have been able to describe with so vivid a minuteness the life she had lived 50 or 60 years before. Perhaps there was a little imagination thrown in — a little invention — a little romancing; or perhaps her character had been so crystalized from the very first that the recounting of its vicissitudes was comparatively easy. My character is not crystalized. So there will be little recorded here that is not transitory; and there will be much here that is quite untrue. The inquisitive reader should he peep between the covers will

---

[1] Elizabeth Grant (1797–1885), Lady Strachey's aunt, who married General Henry Smith and, as Mrs Smith of Baltiboys, wrote *Memoirs of a Highland Lady* which Lady Strachey edited.

find anything but myself, – who perhaps after all do not exist but in my own phantasy. Not to be modest (for this is a private confession – and eaves-droppers must pay the proverbial penalty) – had Shakespeare any character? Of his own, that is to say. Was he not a mere shadow, a mere receptacle for phrases, for faces, for minds, for hearts? All passing away to give place to the next batch. Could he ever have propounded a gospel of his own believing? Did he believe in anything? No, certainly not. Not even, I think, in Right as opposed to Wrong. He was a sceptic, a cynic in his inmost of hearts, swept over and domineered by passions of love; beauty; justice; honour; horror; unutterable woe; calm contentedness. He could never have been a leader of men – mentally, or spiritually, for he was sceptic, and a sceptic is nought. Better so, perhaps; in fact necessarily so. And there are quite sufficient of the other sort.

Among other uses of the diary, I hope it will fulfill the office of safety-valve to my morbidity, which otherwise will become too much to put up with and will have to be abolished. Perhaps however it will only increase it the quicker, and so make a speedy end of itself and me.

When I consider that I am not 18 years of age a shudder passes through my mind and I hardly dare look at the creature those years have made me. Well, perhaps I had better not. It will save a scene.

My life is a turmoil of dulness. My days are spent in a wild excitement over the most arrant details. The putting on of boots is thrilling; the taking off of coat, hat and gloves more so; the walk to the College and back a very procession of agitation. And all carried on with a feverish haste, and a desire to be done with it. As for letters – the expectation of one, no matter from whom is the subject of frenzy.

As usual nothing occurred worth mentioning today. To Coll. in the morning. The usual dulness of Strong:[2] Latin Class, followed by Hebblethwaites[3] excessively penetrating and humourous Greek one. H. is quite a character. Very stout

[2] Professor Herbert Strong.
[3] Assistant Professor P. Hebblethwaites.

and lame of leg; with handsome features and grey beard and hair. His eye-glasses are a constant source of amusement to me: and his continual 'Yes?' which is quite unintended to be answered. Then a hurried bun in the refectory, and Mackay's[4] lecture on Gk. History. This was dull today. M. is rather too much inclined to think himself funny and laugh at his own jokes. He *will* look at me when he means to be witty, which is most inconvenient as I feel that I must smile and yet I do not like pandering. In the afternoon cashed my cheque and proceeded to Young's where I purchased a volume of Shelley's Lyrics – a prospective birthday present for Pernie. En route I passed through Pitt Street, one of the all too common slums of Liverpool. Nearly every street is a slum in this town, except those with the fine shops. Here is nothing intermediate. Hardly anyone lives in the town if they can possibly help it. Pitt Street was painful to me in the extreme; it stank; dirty 'furriners' wandered in groups over it; and a dingy barrel organ rattled its jargon in a yard. Barrel organs are noisome things enough for anyone but he who has nothing else to do but listen to them. To such a one a strain of pleasure is sometimes wafted by those discordant notes. As he listens they assume a grandeur in his mind hitherto undreamt of; they swell with tumultuous and gorgeous harmonies; a great orchestra sways and heaves, booms and falls in his ears; his surroundings are made the temple of a beauty and a wonder; Pitt Street is metamorphosed to a triumphal arcade for a glorious, unearthly procession. The hope of the world, the love, the despair, and the beauty pass along through the squalor, the filth, the desolation of a slum. What a great thing it is to have magnifying glasses always ready to hand, or rather to ear; what a lot we would lose without these valuable adjuncts to existence!

I met an old man today, haggard, and pitiful to behold. His cheeks were a hectic red, and his eyes looked out on me with the weary, desolate expression of one lost and drifting. He tottered along the road in an access of decrepitude, his ragged overcoat clutched over his frail form. But it was not the distress

[4] John Macdonald Mackay, Rathbone Professor of Ancient History.

of poverty or hunger which held him in its grip. The day before I had seen the same old gentleman. He had just nodded a farewell to an even older friend. He stepped along with a sprightly and yet a resolute manner. His clear cut features and beautiful complexion forced themselves on my attention. He was poor, old, weak, but the last thing to be said of him, was that he was unhappy. He answered my gaze with a look of lively speculation tempered with kindness and piety. What did it mean? How did this change come about? Was it a sudden stroke of heart-rending misfortune that snatched the vitality from him in a moment? The death of his wife, or perhaps that of the old friend to whom he had said good-bye so lightly only the day before? Rather must it have been caused by the man's self. He was a spiritual man above all things: spiritual to the exclusion of all else. He was clever-brilliant at College, a splendid career was before him. But he would none of it: his soul was wrapped in the great problems which are only known to souls such as his – problems once taken up never to be solved. But as life goes on the warfare in his breast became less violent. He settled into a cheerfulness only occasionally clouded over. Today a storm broke upon him; he was wracked by the infinite and the inevitable; his spirit heaved amidst a sea of doubts and terrors; he was overwhelmed. Thus it was that I found him this morning and tomorrow, perhaps, he will be well.

Friday March 4th

Naught of interest today as was to be expected. Last night read Ixion in Heaven in bed. I found [it] quite amusing, and not at all vulgar – as it might so easily have been. A good opportunity for vulgarity literally thrown away. Dizzy was personally quite the most interesting man of the last generation; and his career one long drama from beginning to end. He was a link between 2 ages. Born during the first Empire, and 11 years old at the Battle of Waterloo, he died the year I was born – the year of Majuba Hill. I have accepted an invitation to go for a bicycle

ride with Miss Coombe[5] alone, as Dr Stookes will be engaged.
I wonder what will be the result? It took place before, and was
not altogether unsuccessful.

Saturday March 5th

Went out with Miss Coombe bicycling on the Wirral. Started
at ½ past ten, and not home till ½ past 5; thus being out of
doors 7 hours on end. On the whole uneventful enough. Ate
sandwiches on the shore at West Kirby. Bicycled through Park
Gate to Birkenhead. On the way to B who should I pass on a
bicycle but young Marquis whom I had not seen for (I should
think) 6 years. He looked, in the flash I had of him, exactly the
same as ever, though I was surprised to have recognized him. It
seems curious that his brother invited me to go and stay with
him at Birkenhead so many years ago. I wish I had kept up the
acquaintance. But I was young and foolish then, and knew not
the value of friends however humble. I'm afraid I must have
been unkind to him (the elder brother); unkind before I knew
the meaning of the word; unkind before I had had experience
of the great goodness of kindness that was to come. God have
mercy on me! I have his photograph now; but he was not the
only one whom I must have treated badly. There was Bernard
Dodd, the good Dodd, as well; and all 3 have dropped out of
my ken for ever.

In the evening the reading party. *Here*. Only 3 guests turned
up. Mrs Leslie Roberts, the rather nebulous, and perhaps
humourous young wife; Dr Hunt, the honest, hastily-critical
scotchman, and Dr Bradshaw the unsuccessful medical man,
gauche, and very kind. What a party. It went passably,
however. I received an invitation to luncheon with the Nisbets
for Sunday. What, what, will happen? One never knows.

Sunday March 6th

All went well at the Nisbets. The Doctor not home till past 3,

[5] Miss Combe was the headmistress of a large girls' school near by.

so I Madame and the children were the sole party at luncheon. She is really very kind, I *think*; and he, I am sure. Their success, however, has made them rather unbecomingly spiteful on the Stookes; she especially. But what is to be expected? After all, the St's themselves are not quite without their remarks on the Nisbets. Its all rather amusing, and confirms my belief that Doctors are the most jealous, and conceited race on the face of the earth. I don't think I have ever seen a doctor who believed, in reality, in the treatment of any other doctor. Dr. N. talked as he had dinner. He is sympathetic, and has quite the bedside manner. At present all his energies are taken up with *getting on*, and he is succeeding very well. He has brains to attain that end, but I should think not more than that. I should not be surprised if 'Janie' were deteriorating. She is becoming fashionable and already goes to concerts. But at present she is really a good sort, though there are signs of the seeds of evil. I wonder why they married. I am to go to the Pantomime with her and the children next Saturday (D.V.) The children are nice.

Monday March 7th

The weary round again. Prof. R[aleigh] gave a good and sympathetic lecture on Elizabethan Lyrics, with readings. As I was walking down the passage to Strong's lecture room, thinking of the one hour's boredom to be faced there, I thought I heard a shrill and distant cry of 'Mr Strachey'. I did not look round at first, but presently hearing the rustle of a female's approach, I turned and saw a strange figure advancing towards me with signs of recognition. Still I could not guess who it was, till at last the apparition revealed itself as Mrs Raleigh. She looked so very different from what she had about a week ago. So healthy, so pretty. It was with all vagueness that I shook hands with her, and soon she tripped away. My blessings go with you, good woman, good heart. And blessings on the love that you have found and its fruition. To Blurn in the evening.

Tuesday March 8th

Got Mr Raleigh's Robert Louis Stevenson for Pernie. It is quite good, but nothing remarkable, as indeed how could it be. The most interesting things in it are some notes by Hawthorne suggesting plots for stories.

At dinner tonight the conversation turned as usual to Education. I said and think that it is a crying shame and disgrace that Ed. should be in the abominable condition it is. The number of lives wasted is absolutely too much to think of. I am very sleepy. Accepted the dread task of seconding the motion that slang is advisable, for the next debate. Dear me, dear me, what *am* I to say, I wonder? I am very, very sleepy.

Wednesday

Absolument rien.

Thursday March 10th

Had rather a weird experience today riding on my bicycle. After a tour round Sefton Park, and a hunt down Lodge Lane for an apparently fabulous second hand bookshop, I returned home via the loathly Princes Avenue. As I flew my thoughts turned on old Leamington days. Of Suttley's rhyme on me sung by Duchesne etc. I felt a regret for the 'time long past', and murmured to myself a homily on the pleasures of comradeship. As the words passed my lips (for they were half uttered aloud) I heard – or thought I heard – my name called. I was going at a fair pace, and on looking round, only caught a glimpse of the fair face of a youth who was gesticulating at me and speaking. At first I thought it was a mere ordinary joke, but the tone of the voice reminded me strangely of Muirhead major, and the face was not unlike. Could it have been him? It is quite possible, and my surmise is strengthened by the fact that there is a large fishmongers shop here bearing that name. Could it be that the shop owner is an uncle (?) of Muirheads? for I know his father was a hotel-keeper. Well, well, I wonder if I shall ever know, or if it will always remain an unsolved riddle.

As I walked out after tea towards the docks, the sunset over the city gave me an idea (like Culchard) for a sonnet. I did not compose it on the spot, however, but contented myself with repeating rhymes and rythms and gazing on the view. This was really very beautiful – a Turner subject. Birkenhead with the golden sunset behind it and the smoky atmosphere, and the chimneys streaming forth in clouds. Very unsanitary of course, but nevertheless beautiful. There can be no doubt that the worst features of our civilization, the most squalid, filthy, and ugly, are under certain circumstances, rendered truly beautiful. I love you still!

Friday March 11th

To a lecture by Dr S. on Education in Board Schools. Very meandering and vague, but with a good deal of sense in it. What a thing to be able to speak even as well as he does! Right straight on without let or hindrence.

He said today that my taste was not sufficiently catholic, chiefly, I believe, because I averred that I could not put up with Ruskin. He appeared astonished when I told him I had been a devout christian up to the age of 16. To pacify him I said I would read R, and so he had lent me 'Open Sesame', or some such, for my edification. Perhaps I'll be converted to the views he so admirably puts forward. Que sçais-je? Tomorrow with Miss Coombe riding. In the evening to the pantomime with Mrs N. I am dead tired and must totter to bed forthwith.

Saturday March 12th

Last night (Friday) and this morning I read 'Sesame & Lillies'. I really cannot join in St's praise of it. Its remarks on books and words are no doubt sensible, but so stream on and are so over-emphasised, that they become tedious and ridiculous. As for the harangue on the degradation of England etc. etc. ad infinitum, it is difficult to put up with such stuff in patience. It seems to me that R's great fault is wrong-headedness and lack of any sense of proportion. His methods of argument are irritating in the extreme. But I give him credit for putting forth his ideas plainly; who, however, could compare him to Stevenson in any respect whatever?

I have had R.L.S. by W.A.R., and Shelley's Lyrics sent to J.P.S.[6] I hope she has not got them already.

My ride with Miss C. was less tiring than the last and so pleasanter. We went the usual round, and on entering Bhead we encountered a horrible drizzle, which continued to oppress us all the way home. I arrived here dripping. After a diseased meal with Mabel S at 4.30, I was picked up by Mrs Nisbet and reached the Prince o'Wales's at 7.0. The party consisted of myself, Mrs N. and the 2 children. The pantomime was as usual. Enough of the tight waisted fairy prince to make my gorge rise, and of the pumped-up gag to bring a weary smile of recognition to my lips. Eugene Stratton, as a nigger, was the only put-up-able one of the crew. We called Rodney Street on the way back to get a latch key, and poor Dr S. was forced downstairs in his dressing-gown to open the door to me. This was the occasion of much jeering from Janie who called the apparition 'the Stookal dressing-gown'. A most recherche supper at the N's – oysters champaigne etc. And then a walk home to bed, as all the cabs had vanished. I had been invited to dine with them the next day and was unable to refuse.

Sunday March 13th

Walked out to the Nisbets in a hot spring sun. Herbert (?) Hart was there also. He is handsome but pawky. Things lagged rather after dinner; I failed to seize the opportunity for departure; and so I and the children were turned out for a walk in Prince's Gardens. They are really very good children though quite playful and quarrelsome. As we entered Lodge Lane again, who should come up but Dr Dun, – very loud and would-be at his ease. In the drawing-room there were two

[6] Joan Pernel Strachey, Lytton's sister, who was later (1923–41) principal of Newnham College, Cambridge. Walter Raleigh's short essay on Robert Louis Stevenson had been published three years previously.

visitors. One Mrs Ehrenborg whom I had met at a concert previously without knowing her name, the other Miss Silcox the headmistress of the Girls' High School, of whom Pernie had spoken to me. Mrs E. is pretty, with characteristic pince[-]nez. She is I should think nice and perhaps flighty; but women are strange creatures. Miss C. is not so pleasant. She appeared to me to possess the qualities of a groveller, and with P. she had shown herself insolent.

Monday March 14th

The day of the debate on Slang. I was alarmed, as I had only been able to scribble a few remarks by 2.30. The debate was at 4.30, with a tea at 4. I managed to put down some absurd notes and then, palpitating with horror, started off for the College. I arrived late of course. The tea was in the Ladies' Debating Room which was a most charming apartment. I stood dumbly and swallowed a cup of tea. Then, after a long pause while everyone else was talking, we adjourned to the literature room, which was soon pretty well filled. I was horrified to see the swells of the place such as Grundy, Burnett etc accumulated there. Luckily Band began, with the proposition that 'Slang was undesirable', so I came last, seconding Miss Hoare, a lady with flaxen hair and a twang. Fortunately for me I have come to be considered a funny man, so that the audience began to laugh even before I spoke. Perhaps my appearance accounted for this however. I stumbled through my very short oration somehow, and was relieved that it should have gone down so well. The Debate was a weak one and my side lost by 20 to 18. I wonder if the Sphinx will accept my rather inopportune – or at least, unsuitable – contribution. I really don't much care, though I am wildly excited about it. Curious. On Sunday I sketched and wrote down roughly a song on 'Today & tomorrow'. I have since touched it up and it is now lying aside for mature consideration.

Tuesday March 15th

Rain, reading et voila tout! Except the rough sketch of the Birkenhead & Sunset Sonnet. Actually 2 objects for prospective Sphinxes!

Wednesday March 16th

As I passed up Lord Street on my bicycle I saw that one of the Book Shops had a 'selling off' going on and 'Removal of premises' etc. I eagerly rushed to see if there was anything decent, though I had not over much 'cash' to spare. I saw nothing of any interest but a Byron – in fact two Byrons: one large, and probably, I surmised, complete; t'other small, and probably, I concluded extracted. I went in boldly; my surmise was correct. The large one was pub. by Murray 1837 and was called at any rate complete. The small one was a ratlike edition of extracts – foul! How any one could ever buy an extract of an author, I can't conceive; that is to say to buy an extract and nothing more. I refused the 1/4d and took (rather extravagantly) the 2/6d. The shopman kindly urged me to purchase 'this beautiful edition of Boswell's life of Johnson – the best biography ever written; – yes, I assure you, the best biography ever written.' It was the most disgusting sight conceivable, with *hideous* pictures in; in 4 loathsome volumes, bound in that particularly repulsive flabby cloth. I passed away from it into the inner shop. There were some valuable books, well bound. Among other things I saw 'Lady Lytton – A Vindication' and 'Fables in Song' which I should much like to possess. I then departed leaving Lord B. to be sent up. Much to my annoyance, however, he did not arrive in the evening as I expected.

Thursday March 17th

Nor did I find him on coming down this morning; but a letter from P. which pleased me. Thanks for the gifts and the address in Germany, where she goes with a semi German Jewess, whom Pippa called Miss Dreyfus. Found my Lord awaiting me on my return from C. He is fat, heavy and dirty. But really not at all bad I think. At any rate *tolerably* complete – as of course the very latest verses to be issued in the new edition are not included. I think I shall have the Noble Lord rebound, as his binding is the dirtiest part of him, though quite nice if it was not dirty. I began Sardanapalus today. I must say the subject is very interesting to me – not interesting – *thrilling*, dramatic. The falling away of a great empire. Omar's few lines on the subject in his History of Greece are *good*. Quel homme, ce Byron!

Friday March 18th

Professor Carey[7] after his lecture today asked me to lunch with him some day or other, and go out for a walk afterwards. I accepted but no day has been settled yet. I wonder what he is like: very kind I should think, and I expect he asks various students to lunch with him as a matter of duty. I had no opportunity of asking Prof. Raleigh for the Riddle, a thing I have been intending to do for the last 3 weeks. I really must, however, the next time I see him. Tomorrow a bicycle ride with Miss C. and perhaps Dr St.

Saturday March 19th

A muddy drizzly day was waiting for me when I looked out of window this morning. Too horrible for bicycling, I thought. I therefore went round to Miss C. to ask her if she agreed. She had had no thought of riding on such a day but proposed the Arts & Crafts Exhibition. Though I had been before I was willing to go again, and so, after inspecting some engravings (2 by Piranesi) which had been given to the school, we started off. Her criticisms were, I thought, good and sensible, though rather naively given. Among other things that we looked at were some designs for stained-glass windows. She said her 'artist-sister' had made some beautiful designs of this sort,

[7] Professor Frank Carey, a mathematical don.

which had been among the best things at the London Arts &
Crafts a year or two ago. 'Yes', she heard someone at the
exhibition say 'those are by Miss Coombe, you know, who is
going to marry Mr Fry. He's such a good and nice young man –
I hope she's good enough for him!' 'Any relation of Fry's
Chocolate?' said I. 'A nephew!' 'Oh, because I know a
nephew, an artist'. 'Yes, Roger'! So Miss Coombe's brother-
in-law is Roger Fry! Who'd ha' thought it? And I suppose
Oliver must know her sister. Well, well, its all very weird!

In the afternoon my head ached rather, and I sat disconso-
late. Enter Dr S. He talked vaguely and then sat down. What is
the meaning of this I thought. There he sat, pretending to read,
when I hovered vaguely. 'Is it going to be a repetition of the
Mabel incident'? I thought. But no, in about ten minutes out he
went. At tea time, Mrs Stookes entered from an outing. 'Have
you heard the news?' she said 'Has Elshie told you?' 'No' said
Elshie, 'I haven't told him a word'. I was mad with anxiety to
know what it was, especially as I was told it concerned me. At
last the Doctor said 'We're going to have a dentist downstairs'.
This did not convey much to me at first, but soon I gathered
that one creature more was going to take up his abode here.
His partial abode. He is to come at 9 and go away at 5, using
Dr S's consulting room for his patients. 'But where are you
going?' I asked. 'Into your room'. I was perfectly stolid. Mrs S.
was conciliatory at once. 'Oh no, no Elshie, and of course its
not settled yet, and we thought you might go into the nursery'.
I said I should be delighted, but questioned the wisdom of the
plan. But of course £150 a year is not to be despised. It must
have come in the nick of time – this offer. They were evidently
tottering to decay, their bills coming in, new clothes wanted,
and nothing to eat. They have been forced to accept the dentist.
Another maid is to be got to open the door for his patients.
'And where', I asked 'are these streams of people to wait?'

'Yes, I hope Doctor Dun won't mind,' said Madam. 'But I
shouldn't think he would – just breakfast and luncheon in his
room – that's all! 'And if he does', said Monsieur, 'he'll have to
go that's all'. So the dining-room is to be turned to waiting-
room! 'He's been rather tiresome lately, and I think I shall ask

him to go'. Mrs S. procured a respite. It was subsequently settled with much talking and measuring that I 'am to be left in peace' and Dr S. is to make the Day Nursery his consulting-room. The reason for this is that if I went into the Nursery and Dr S. into here, both rooms would have to be done up, but now, my room can very well be left as it is. Doubtless also they thought that 'Lady Strachey' might be annoyed. But they gave no reason at all.

I have finished the Ordeal of Richard Feverel. It is excellent. But it needs rereading, so I have begun again. There is a good deal that's unexplained in it – to my mind, but of course it is *charming*. I think it wants unity; taking it chapter by chapter, nothing could be better; as a whole, I am doubtful.

Sunday March 20th

A lazy morning. In the afternoon walked down to the docks and thence to the landing stage. The crowds of people were appalling. The landing stage blocked; and *all* hideous. It gave me the shivers in two minutes and I fled. My self-conscious vanity is really most painful. As I walk through the streets I am agonised by the thoughts of my appearance. Of course it is hideous, but what *does* it matter? I only make it worse by peering into people's faces to see what they are thinking. And the worst of it is I hate myself for doing it. The truth is I want *companionship*. Miss C. is not good enough, besides I want someone who can go out for walks with me at any time. Barkway? Dear me, is that all University College can give me? If I could only make friends with Grundy or Bird! But my 'habitual reserve' is too much for them. Well, well, well, perhaps I shall find someone some day. And then I am sure he – or she – will *not* belong to University College. Talking of shes, I think it is too much that one cannot speak to a member of 'the sex' without being looked upon askance by somebody or other. If only people were more sensible on this point, half the so called immorality would come to an end at once. I wonder if I shall ever 'fall in love'. I can't help smiling at the question – if they only knew – if they only knew! But it is a tragedy also.

Monday March 21st

Urged myself out today to pay some calls. Bought a pair of gloves; put on my thick *blue* trousers: and marched. First to the Nisbets to return Prince Otto, and write a note to the Dr about the certificate of illness. Then to the Booths. Hurray! Not at home. Then in horror to the Holts 'Is Mrs Holt in?' 'Oh yes, she's *in*!' was the peculiar reply. I was ushered into the Drawing Room. 'Mr Straschhieezy' 'Mr Who?' said Mrs Holt on the sofa 'Mr Strachedy' was the still ambiguous answer. 'Oh! Mr Strachey! You ought never to have been allowed in.' To cut the matter short it turned out that the youngest daughter had had scarlet fever, and that although all was safe, no visitors were allowed. Rather strange altogether. She jabbered, I grinned. And that was the end of the visit. I came home to find Mrs Boulnois in the drawing room. Her china blue eyes are superb. She said that she had seen my mother, and that she was going to a party there on Tuesday week, which was news to me. She also said something about a ball at which, when Mrs St told Dr St, the latter was surprised and pained. 'What! A ball in lent! Impossible you must be mistaken. A ball in lent! She *couldn't* go to one. etc.' Really can people be so idiotic?

Tuesday

Examinations begin today. Death to me of course. Greek. A letter from Miss C asking for a bicycle ride. No letter from the Gate. Which is beginning to annoy me, the last I had was on M. 2nd. The examination went off peacably. In the evening I threw Latin to the winds and concentrated myself on History. This wise, I think.

Wednesday 23rd

Latin and History Examinations. In the morning a letter enclosing £2 10 for journey etc. In the afternoon Mrs Stookes told me that the Booths wanted me to go to dinner with them and to the Wellington Rooms afterwards. It was only by accident that I learnt it was a ball. The ball in lent! I was horrified of course. Went round Sefton Park with Miss Coombe in a violent wind. Returned dead tired to Blum[8] who, I must say, let me off easy. Prepared for English Literature Examination.

Thursday March 24th

Prepared for English Literature Examination up to the last moment. Half an hour before it began I *luckily* borrowed Eastwood's notebook, and learnt a thousand things. As it was it was bad enough. Could not concentrate attention.

In afternoon bought a pair of white kid gloves and a tie, and then went to tea with Miss C. She was rather irritating. I departed in a snow storm, ordering a cab en route. Of course the cab did not come at half past seven as I ordered, and mad with horror I had to start off walking. Fortunately I caught a hansom in Duke Street, and reached the Booths in good time. I entered a crowded drawing room. Shook hands with Mrs Booth, Mr Booth, Harriet, Hilda and Alfred. Then – 'Mr Strachey – the Dean of Ely'. I sat down next to Hilda Boulnois and received the first snub of the evening! 'I hope you grasped we were going to a ball, Mr Strachey!' Yes. 'Because it would have been so inconvenient if you'd forgotten gloves or anything of that sort!' Thank the Lord, I had not *this* time.

At dinner sat between Brenda and Mabel Booth, and had to talk to both, which was especially tedious as I wanted to listen to what the Dean was saying to Madame. He turned out to have been an intimate friend of Papa's, and the tutor of Charlie and Arthur.[9] I was not particularly surprised. He is a remarkably handsome man, with a cast of face rather in the mould of Leighton's and the proper ecclesiastical long iron grey hair. The impression given by his conversation with Mrs

[8] Dr Blum was 'a Swede, and decent enough' who was supervising a course of strengthening exercises for Strachey – 'movements of the arms, legs and body, he presses in the opposite direction' – three days a week.

[9] The second and third sons of John Strachey, a younger brother of Sir Richard Strachey.

Booth I overheard was not altogether pleasant. He jeered for a long time at Mrs Creighton, which I thought unnecessary and commonplace, and altogether gave me the idea of what Mrs Boulnois would call a 'worldly' man. But apparently I am wrong. He is a socialist. In an omnibus to the Wellington Rooms. They are very fine; built in Waterloo year, and belonging to a club who give about 5 or 6 dances a year. There was a great crowd of people. Many had come up for the Grand National of next day, and may be judged accordingly. I managed to get along somehow. Everyone was very kind. I saw Robert Holt and a daughter but did not accost them. As I watched the mob my eye caught a very broad muscular man, handsome and in rather a pet. A woman followed him. I was on the alert long before I felt any definite reason. The man was clearly of a different cast from the majority of those present, for he was nonchalant enough to display his temper openly. A suspicion of a memory gave me a clue. Yes, his ears were the same! Could it be – possibly – Harold Suttley's brother, the cricketer? I wonder. I had only seen him for a short time – and yet . . . Well it *was*. I found his name on the visitor's list afterwards. Mr A. M. Suttley. Mr A. M. Suttley. I remember how I said to Hanbury I thought he was the luckiest man in the world. Handsome, strong, with a beautiful wife who was at the same time an heiress! He had gone before I could look at him again. It was with all clumsiness that I managed to procure a cab for Boulnois et cie; and with all joy that I marched homeward at the comparatively early hour of half past one in the morning. After all it didn't matter much. The only thing of importance being the fact that I had given my cabman half a crown instead of a penny. Well, well.

Friday March 25th

Breakfast in bed. In the afternoon the last weary Examination. The dentist's things are moving slowly into the house, to the jeers of the St's. The last day of term. The Sphinx[10] arrived. I

---

[10] *The Sphinx* was a university magazine at Liverpool. Strachey had sent in a verse 'On being asked for a description of a Roundel' which was later published in *The Granta* after he had gone up to Cambridge.

tore it open. No. Not accepted. As I thought. How else could
be interpreted the frowns of Grundy and the smiles of Bird?

SUMMER TERM

Thursday April 21st

Arrived in time for Mackay's lecture at 12.30. Afterwards he
summoned all those in the 1st division into his room, and gave
us each others papers to correct. Bicycled to the Stookes. As I
entered my room they rose from a table on which were spread
the remains of luncheon. Nothing was said on this subject,
however.

6

CAMBRIDGE ALTERED THE *whole tenor of Strachey's life. The congenial atmosphere, with its high percentage of vocational bachelors, liberated him from the Victorian climate of Lancaster Gate in a far deeper way than Rothiemurchus had done, and for years Cambridge became for him a home from home. Within a short time of going up to Trinity College in the Michaelmas Term of 1899 he had made many new and permanently valuable friendships that were to form the basis of the Bloomsbury Group — with, among others, Clive Bell, E. M. Forster, Thoby Stephen, Saxon Sydney-Turner and Leonard Woolf.*

From a withdrawn, socially timid individual, with congenital short-sight, startlingly pale complexion and long limp body, Strachey developed a determined character that left its mark on at least three generations of undergraduates. From his deficiencies, his very lack of vitality, he created a personality of strange force. Under the inspired tension of his silence the very fires would seem to fade into ashes, the birds stop singing on the trees.

The year 1902, in which two of the following short pieces were written, marks a watershed in Strachey's writings and opinions. It was in the spring of this year that he was elected to the secret Cambridge Conversazione Society known as the 'Apostles', and this brought him into contact with such men as Desmond MacCarthy, Ralph Hawtrey, G. E. Moore and Bertrand Russell. Using what he needed from Moore's Principia Ethica *(aesthetic experience + personal relations =*

the good life), Strachey took the nineteenth-century cult of homosexuality and turned it into a weapon of twentieth-century revolt. As his Apostolic 'First and Last Will and Testament' illustrates, he intended to amuse the converted and shock the unconverted, especially by his antagonism to Christianity and the worldly religion of success.

His dialogue in the Trinity diary was with either G. M. Trevelyan, the historian, or his younger brother R. C. Trevelyan, the poet, both of whom were Apostles. Since Strachey almost always refers to R. C. Trevelyan as 'Bob Trevy', the Trevelyan in question is probably the historian. Despite a lifetime of politeness, Noël Annan wrote, G. M. Trevelyan 'loathed Strachey and his works'. The two of them had a long-drawn-out battle on the subject of Apostolic homosexuality, in which, Bertrand Russell recorded, 'Lytton Strachey was on the whole victorious'.

There is no specific date to 'Examination Papers in Sex Education', which may have been written after Strachey left university. If so, it was probably conceived on a return visit there, for in mood and tone it undoubtedly belongs to the Cambridge period.

FIRST AND LAST
WILL AND TESTAMENT

I, GILES LYTTON STRACHEY (servant & plenipotentiary in Christ) being in my right mind & body, do hereby make away, deliver, give, bequeath, & present.

(1)   My soul, to the Devil.

(2)   My body, to the head superintendent of the Cavendish laboratory (anatomical branch) on condition that it shall be duly dissected, articulated, & wired, upon the table lately employed by Dr McTaggart[1] during his lectures.

(3)   The goodwill of my privacies, to God and the heirs male of his body lawfully begotten, in default of issue to The Holy Ghost for life, and on his demise to the Absolute, as tenants in common, in fee simple.

(4)   My glasses, mind, & chaise percée to the Ghost of Voltaire, or Mr Morley.

(5)   My sense of humour to the next Bishop of Oxford.

(6)   My nose (if it be celluloid) to John Tresidder Sheppard,[2] scholar of King's College in Cambridge, in memory of the one that wasn't.

(7)   My alchemic coffee-pot to Herr Eesdaile, on condition he wears nothing but it during one year in each day.

(8)   My future tragedies to the Society for the Promotion of Christian Knowledge.

(9)   My autobiography to the British Museum, signed and sealed, & not to be opened for 300 years.

[1] J. E. McTaggart, the Hegelian philosopher, who was an Apostle.

[2] (Sir) John Sheppard was later Provost of King's College, Cambridge, 1933–54.

(10)   My treatise on syphilis to Dr Cunningham,[3] & on his demise to my last hospital nurse & wife.

(11)   My literary remains other than my autobiography to the remaining members of the Trinity.

(12)   The Man of Kineth to Mr Gascoigne Machie.

(13)   My notes on the Intellectual Revival to Mr Gashon.

(14)   My fallacies, if, after distribution of the aforesaid bequests, there be found any remaining to Sire Hawtrey.

(15)   My racehorses to the Cambridge Conversazione Society.

(16)   My sins to our blessed Saviour, most redoubtable lord, and eternal governor, Jesus Christ, to whom be ascribed all might, majest[y], power & dominion in specula speculorum.

Witnesses
Leonard Sidney Woolf
Ralph George Hawtrey
Saxon Arnold Sydney-Turner
                    AMEN
          Delivered under our hand & seal
          this 21st of November
          in the year of Grace
                    1902 Giles Lytton Strachey.

[3] Dr William Cunningham, known as 'Parson Bill', the economic historian who became Strachey's director of studies, and later turned down his fellowship dissertation.

THE TRINITY DIARY NOV 1902

NOV 26th 1902

I lunched with Trevelyan at 1.30. He had been invited to our dance.

T. Do you like dancing very much?

I. Oh no, not at all.

T. Nor do I, and I shall be out of town.

I. How does one dance? I can never understand how anyone ever manages it. The nerve!

T. The important thing about dancing is that it brings the sexes into closer physical contact than is allowed by the conventions of society on any other occasion.

I. Really?

T. My dear man, didn't you know that? That is why rather stupid mothers who don't understand or don't like really good intellectual conversation think that giving dances is the best way of getting their daughters married.

I. Very interesting. The contact question never struck me before.

T. I'm surprised to hear you say that. The other night at the Society I thought you said you were only in love with people physically.

I. Oh, but with men.

T. Is that all?

I. That's all.

T. How old are you?

I. I'm not quite sure.

T. Twenty-three? Well, tell me that again when you're

twenty-six. I've known so many men who were just the same. We do everything later now. We grow up later, we fall in love later, we die later (among other things). In three years you'll be completely changed.

I.   You give one hope.

T.   That is really the good side of University Life. Men come up here for three years to do hard intellectual work; and they can concentrate all their energies on that. The sexual question doesn't come into it at all. It's one of the best facts in modern English life that there are no women at University.

I was silent, not venturing a combustion, and we passed on to Brown, where the combustion inevitably came.

T.   Have you seen Brown lately?

I.   I saw him last night (He must have known this, and that's why he asked me to lunch).

T.   What do you think of him?

I.   I think he's very nice. (Moore's admirable word.)

T.   You ought to elect him at once.

I.   I don't think at once. He might be so very much improved.

T.   But wouldn't he be improved by the Society? Everyone has been.

I.   Then I suppose everyone ought to be elected.

T.   If everyone's like Brown.

Examination Papers
in Sex Education

I – *Elementary*

1. Describe the reproductive system of the periwinkle.
2. Explain the meaning of (a) 'in heat', (b) 'the rutting season', (c) 'to serve the mare', (4) 'covered by the old goat'.
3. Write a short biography of Oedipus.
4. 'When the hens are away, the cocks will play.' Illustrate this.
5. What do you understand by 'the language of flowers'?

II – *For Higher Forms*

1. Distinguish clearly, with diagrams, between the clitoris and the vagina.
2. Comment upon the following, paraphrasing where necessary, and giving names of authors—
   (a) 'I have forgotten,' said my Father, 'to wind up the clock.'
   (b) 'They make our hairs, and you our flesh, upright.'
   (c) 'Thy prophet, thy preacher, thy poet,
       Sin's child by incestuous Death.'
   (d) 'Mais une, entre autres, me troubla.'
   (e) 'To know her was a liberal education.'
   (f) 'Paedicabo vos et irrumabo.'
   (g) 'The emerald penis of a gay baboon.'
3. What do you know of Giton, Anactoria, Sir Charles Dilke, la Duchesse de Berry, le Marquis de Sade?
4. 'Plato, we have no doubt, was a much better man than

Sir George Etherege. But Plato has written things at which
Sir George Etherege would have shuddered.' Discuss this.
5. Write a short essay on
   either Shakespeare's Sonnets, psycho-pathologically
   considered.
   or The history of French Letters.

III – *Advanced*. (If the Essay is chosen, not more than 3 other
                   questions should be attempted.)
1. Trace the connections between Sadism and Masochism,
with examples from history, or from cases privately known.
2. In your opinion, what is the influence of masturbation
upon (1) men, (2) women, (3) the higher quadrupeds, (4) the
human race?
3. Elucidate, on the basis of Dr Freud's teaching,
   (a) The Conversion of St Paul.
   (b) The Channel Tunnel project.
   (c) The European War.
   (d) The growing popularity of tooth-picks in the United
       States.
4. Bestiality: should it be encouraged? And if not, why not?
5. What evidence of inversion can you point to in the works
of
   either (a) Sophocles
   or   (b) Rupert Brooke?
6. Subjects for an essay. (One only to be chosen.)—
Anus *v.* Vagina. The Influence of the Stool upon Social
Institutions. The Pleasures of a Single Life. Dr Freud,
analysed by himself.

7

IN THE SUMMER of 1905 Strachey retreated to Great Oakley Hall, a large country house six miles from Kettering, which his family had rented for the holidays. He was working hard over his long dissertation on Warren Hastings, but had little hope of it earning him a Trinity fellowship. 'My dissertation oppresses me horribly,' he told Clive Bell (28 July 1905). 'But I cast it off as much as I can.' And to Maynard Keynes he confessed: 'I spend hours, days, and weeks simply staring at blank sheets of paper – hopeless, helpless, utterly incompetent, completely vague, absolutely comatose, physically, morally and spiritually, DEAD.'

He was resurrected two days later by the arrival of his 'wonderfully nice, and nice looking' cousin, Duncan Grant. The fevered effusion he poured out on 6 August records his impressions of Duncan Grant, whose brief visit, he told Keynes (3 August), was like a glimpse of heaven. 'I want to go into the wilderness of the world, and preach an infinitude of sermons on one text – "Embrace one another". It seems to me the grand solution . . . I am cloudy, I fear almost sentimental. But I'll write again. Oh yes, it's Duncan. He's no longer here, though; he went yesterday to France. Fortunate, perhaps, for my dissertation.'

Fortunately, perhaps, for his literary career, the dissertation failed to win him a fellowship.

AUG 6th 1905

FOUR DAYS AGO he left me, and since then I have had time to reflect on what has happened. How absurdly I used to imagine the enjoyment I might get from him, perhaps, if I were to try! I pictured myself in my chair at Cambridge, in front of the fire, with all the heavy luxury of that winter atmosphere about me. He was to be sitting on the floor, with his hands before the blaze, and his head between my thighs, so that I could stroke his hair, whenever I might wish, with both my hands. Yes! he was to be an object to play with, a delightful object, but an object of lust. But, when the moment actually came, when, in the orchard, in the sunshine, in the summer morning, I really found that he was mine to hold and to caress, oh! how different were my feelings then! I was entranced. I was overcome, and, even now, as I remember it, I am filled with a mysterious and almost dreadful joy, – not by the consummation of my own poor pleasure, the satisfaction of the desires that I had so vaguely dreamed, but by the sudden knowledge that he too was moved, that he too was strangely happy, that his hands were clasping me, that his arms were drawing me towards him, that his head was bent upon my breast. For the first time, I loved his soul.

In the future, when we meet, I want to be worthy of what I felt then, of what I am feeling now. I want our intercourse to be unmarred by the weaknesses that I know are mine too often. I want him to love me as I love him, and to deserve his love. Let me stand erect in my own self-consciousness, in that he may find in my strength the splendour that I find in his beauty; and

118

let us be occupied with the cleansing aspirations of our art as much as with each other and with ourselves. Thus only shall we learn to laugh together in our happiness, and, in our agony, to divide our tears.

8

'AFTER CAMBRIDGE, BLANK, *blank, blank,*' *Strachey wrote to Leonard Woolf. He now re-entered what he called 'the limbo of unintimacy' – family life, Lancaster Gate. The next five years were a black period in his life. Nor was this mitigated when in the late summer of 1907 the Stracheys moved to Number 67 Belsize Park Gardens, Hampstead. His illnesses and complaints multiplied alarmingly – even the weather was unfair; his writings brought nothing about, his lovers seemed all untrue. He dashed hopefully back and forward between London and Cambridge, with recuperative spells on the Continent. He even proposed marriage to Virginia Stephen who, to his alarm, briefly accepted him. It was the ultimate failure.*

But he was not idle. He wrote almost eighty reviews for the Spectator, *and a number of literary and biographical essays for the* Independent Review, *the* Albany Review *and the* New Quarterly.

1910 marked a turning-point in his life. It was in this year that he was commissioned to write Landmarks in French Literature, *and it was now, too, that he got to know Ottoline Morrell and Henry Lamb who together liberated him from Bloomsbury, as Moore had previously released him from Victorianism. For a time, Strachey was infatuated with both Ottoline and Lamb, hardly able to distinguish between the attractions of each. They propelled him into a superbly bohemian world – the chaotic and spontaneous world of Augustus John, Epstein and the Russian mosaicist Boris Anrep.*

Strachey's tendency was to fall in love with the sort of person he would like to have been. During this period of obscurity, he wished to be an artist – a literary artist, it would have to be. He hoped also to fill the place in his affections partly vacated by Duncan Grant with the bewitching figure of Henry Lamb.

DIARY – 1910

Monday, February 28th

Began R.[1]

Tuesday, March 1

The Triple Bill. Went with MCS[2] & Ethel. An hour too early.
Virginia gave me 2/6d for a birthday present. Went to O's[3] in a
taxi with her, Vanessa & Norton.[4] Very amusing. Talked
bawdy to Virginia who was extremely beautiful. At O's saw
Henry Lamb for the first time for ages. Looked ill but
extraordinarily attractive. Talked to him and he was very
agreeable. Went away with D[uncan] late, and kissed him on
the stairs. Walked with him to Russell Square excited and
happy, then took a taxi which was paid for by Virginia's 2/6d.

Thursday, March 3

Aft. Walked with D. to Heath, where he painted. Went to
Rothensteins. Malaise, but interesting. Fitzroy Sq. very dull.

[1] 'R' may possibly refer to Rousseau. Strachey's essay 'The Rousseau Affair'
written in 1907, was published in May 1910 in the *New Quarterly*.

[2] Marjorie Colville Strachey, Lytton's younger sister.

[3] Lady Ottoline Morrell.

[4] Vanessa Bell, the artist and sister of Virginia Woolf, who married Clive Bell;
and Harry Norton, the mathematical don at Trinity to whom *Eminent
Victorians* is dedicated.

Monday, March 7

Tea party at O's to meet Madame Rammay, who didn't come. Lady Henry C-Bentinck, Lady Alicia, Pearsall Smith, Miss Sechel, Adrian [Stephen], O's new picture by H.[5]

Tuesday, March 8

Went to O's with D. 10.30 H. there, & Eddie,[6] few others. No Bloomby. Talked to D, and then with O and a tiresome giant. Eddie came up, raving about H, with whom he'd been talking. I became very much bored, saw D & H talking near the door, got up and went to them. Told H. I'd been to see him. 'Why did you come?' 'Oh, to make love to you'. Then went off with them both, and walked along Tottenham Ct. Rd flirting violently. Arranged to go and be drawn by H. on Friday.

Wednesday, March 9

Aft. Tried to make D. undress. Said he'd wait till the summer. Tea with D. at Savile.
Madras House. D. in gallery.

Thursday, March 10

Dinner at Gordon Sq. Complaints of Clive as to collective affectation and dullness of set. 'Everyone tries to make his individuality tell' I couldn't believe it. He refused to go to Fitzroy. I went with Vanessa. Ianthe there. Also D. MCS & Tudor Castle. O came & Lady Beatrice. I failed to make headway with O, and soon went. Adrian very amiable – especially, I thought, to me. Began to rag, as I was going, and followed me out and ragged me in the hall. As we were ragging, Turner[7] and H. came in. I was delighted and went off quite happy.

[5] Henry Lamb.
[6] Eddie Marsh.
[7] Saxon Sydney-Turner.

Friday, March 11

Visit to H at 4 oc. A good deal surprised and very much interested. Talked a great deal, and played, and drew me. Touched his cheek without annoyance. Excited when I came away. After dinner went to Sangers with J.[8] Virginia there. Also Miss Mayor, Smythe and others. Walked with V. & J. to a taxi, wh. she insisted on taking. Charming in cab. She said she'd left Adrian and D. on the floor, struggling. 'I couldn't wait to see how it would end.' When she got out she gave 10/- to J to pay for the cab, and so we rattled home.

Saturday, March 12

Finished Ch. 2 of R.
Aft. D came for 5 minutes to tell me about Adrian. Very futile. A. so wonderful. Esp. when D. announced his feelings. I said 'What did he say?' D. 'Nothing; that was what was so wonderful.' Announced his dep for Const. with Pozzo[9] on Thursday. I was intensely depressed. Tea with Virginia. J. caustic on Adrian & D.

Sunday, March 13

After tea walked with J. to Fitzroy Sq. Found H. there, & D walked up. Walked to H's, and went up with D. H. played. I began to feel bored, and at last went, leaving them together.

Monday, March 14

Invitation with D. Walk on Heath. Morning. Thoughts of Salisbury. Tea at Savile with J. Hopes of seeing D. after dinner. Nothing. Almost decide on Salisbury.

---

[8] James, Lytton's younger brother.
[9] John Maynard Keynes. He and Duncan Grant were about to leave for Constantinople on holiday.

Tuesday, March 15

Appearance of D – while still in bed. Had stayed the night. Locked out of Fellows Rd. I said 'Really' and went to sleep again. In morning went to Gordon Sq. to ask Clive to come to Salisbury – couldn't. Vanessa also there. I suggested Adrian. They thought he might go. Went to Fitzroy and asked Adrian. He refused, engagements for Opera, wondered why I was going – 'mad, quite mad'. I went away rather chilled. Still uncertain at Belsize. At last decided, & told JMS.[10] Pernel arr. from C. to lunch. Said she would follow if I liked. Train 3.30 from Waterloo. Platform crowded with cadets returning to Osborne. As I was walking about looking at the beautiful creatures, Noland suddenly appeared with Connie seeing off his son, who was one of them.
The Old George Inn.
The Cathedral and Close.
Wrote to Clive, JBS:[11] and H[enry].

Wednesday, March 16

Arr. of J.P.S.[12]
Wilton.
Wrote to D[uncan].

Thursday, March 17

Letters from JBS, Clive and H.
The Race Course.

Friday, March 18

Dep. of D. for Const.
Return from Salisbury.

---

[10] Jane Maria Strachey, Lytton's mother.
[11] James Beaumont Strachey, Lytton's younger brother.
[12] Joan Pernel Strachey.

Saturday, March 19

Lunch with Mr Etheridge at Savile. Sensitive and faded.
Walked through Bond St to H. He drew me. Semi-rag: I tried to
embrace him. Extreme severity. 'Absolutely out of the question, impossible'. I was bitterly disappointed. Managed at last
to discuss. 'Not enraged in the least – but only wanted to draw
me.' I said. 'You knew I was a dangerous character'. He said 'I
hoped to draw you first'. Eventually he admitted he'd perhaps
been brutal. Should I come again? At last I said I would. As I
went he said 'It's just like Ottoline'.
Dinner at Gordon Sq. Very agreeable. Clive almost sympathetic. News of Virginia's illness.

Sunday, March 20

Aft. Walked with J[ames] to heath, looking at houses.

Monday, March 21

Postcard from George[13] at Florence, with Botticelli youth,
suggesting I should go and see him in Paris. Wrote to him.
Letter from Rupert to J saying he could go on reading party.
Dep. of JMS for Norfolk.

Tuesday, March 22

After lunch, arrival of J. from [*Spectator*] office with news that
he could not be spared and so reading party impossible.
Walked across Regent's Park to Savile. Tea and meeting to
decide on paid secretary. Alfred Plowden[14] in chair. Stanford
disgusting. Johnny Atkins seen. Spoke to Alf. and J. Pollock.
Dinner, sat next Basil Hammond.
Taxi to the Russells' in Ashley Gardens. A furnished flat full of

[13] George Mallory, the mountaineer.
[14] Alfred Plowden, a first cousin of Lady Strachey's was a magistrate at
Marylebone Police Court and a tremendously celebrated figure in the popular
press.

virgins. Mrs Rothenstein[15] an exception. Talked to her, Miss Mackail and Miss Lamb. Appearance of O. with Philip and H. Failed to make progress with O. Talked to H, who was agreeable, and divine in evening dress. An unexpected excitement. But why so many virgins?

Wednesday, March 23

R. in morning.
Aft. Walked to heath and back by Highgate pond. Randy poster on way up.
After dinner Turner appeared. Talked of H's visit Cambridge. Declared we had all (especially Woolf) maltreated him — except him. Story of his going into Walter's[16] outer room, and hearing him & H. discussing us in the inner dining room, and his gliding silently away again. Very typical that he should never have told it before.

Thursday, March 24

Walked to H. 4 oc. Appearance of O. in a purple hat. H & I walked to buy buns in Tottenham Ct. Rd. He takes off his hat to a cabbage-selling woman. Tries to persuade me to go into pubs and drink vermouth. Had been drunk the day before — pure pleasure. Met John's 2nd son[17] when drunk, as beautiful as ever. He drew me twice. His room charming. Rugs, stuffs and flowers from O. Discussion of Walter's character. I suggested he was a eunuch, he on the whole agreed. Asked if D was one. Description of visit to Cambridge. Visite discrète. Announced his dep. to O's cottage on Sat.
Dinner at Gordon Sq. Clive very fat. Discussion as to whether sods. were *a priori* better than womanisers. Very dull. Read

[15] Alice Knewstub had been an actress before her marriage to (Sir) William Rothenstein.

[16] (Sir) Walter Lamb, elder brother of Henry Lamb, who became secretary of the Royal Academy.

[17] Augustus John's second son, (Sir) Caspar, had had his seventh birthday two days beforehand. He later became Admiral of the Fleet.

'Some day'. Told Clive about O. He said she had pretended to be going on Wed. night. Q. How far?
Dep. of Peter for Ireland.
Headache in morning.

Friday, March 25

Walked to H. in afternoon and asked him to come to dinner. He came. J & I only others. Appeared hungry. After dinner J played Hammerclavier on pianola. Left alone we talked intimement about ourselves. Atmosphere of demi-flirtation, but infinitely discreet.
Dep. of MCS for Florence.
R. in morning.

Saturday, March 26

Dep. of JPS for Florence.
—Bloomsbury for Studland.
—H for O.
J & I to Dollar Princess in evening. Appalling.
R in morning.
Ob. C. D. Robertson.

Sunday, March 27

Went with J to Harrow, whence we walked to Pinner. Tea in an inn, and returned by train.

9

BY MARCH 1913, *Strachey had published* Landmarks in French Literature, *almost* finished Ermyntrude and Esmeralda, *his pornographic entertainment for Henry Lamb, and had begun contributing essays to the* Edinburgh Review. *The idea of* Eminent Victorians *was already stirring in his mind and he believed, intermittently, that if he could find some cottage in the country and furnish it comfortably, he might live and work in comparative happiness. Much of the winter of 1912–13 he spent at Lockeridge, near Marlborough, with the politican and writer Hilton Young 'my main prop in life' who tramped the country with him in his quest for rustic sanctuary.*

Their search was fruitless, and since he was apprehensive about starting Eminent Victorians *in such unsettled circumstances, Strachey decided to postpone matters by realizing a long-cherished dream – to go for two months on a grand tour of France and Italy. He would return in the early summer, bankrupt, but bursting with health and buoyancy, and straining to be at his work again.*

He set off alone on 16 March. The account of his voyage from Folkestone to Boulogne was written on the train between Boulogne and Paris later that same day.

MARCH 8, 1913

THE GYPSIES IN THE FIELD. (Evening.)

A row of three sordid little huts along the top of a field – made of red-brown canvas stretched across so as to make tent-like-coop-like little erections – very small and hunched, with smoke coming out. The canvas full of holes, and children looking through. Chattering and singing inside. As we passed on the way up, two boys came out and looked at us – one very pretty and engaging. Coming back, a girl appeared outside one of the huts and shouted to know the time. (Did she want to know it?) And a face looking through one of the holes asked for a copper with hardly any conviction. The two young men came walking quickly up from the bottom of the field. The two boys were near the huts and began calling out to them. – 'Come here! Come here I say, or I'll break your jaw for you.' It was their way of showing their delight at seeing the young men. Then they ran to meet them, and the smaller of the two took hold of one of the young men's coats and ran along behind him; the bigger boy gave a curvet when he came up to them, and ran along by the side and just a little in front. The young men smiled, but otherwise paid no attention at all, and walked on towards the huts. Then a lot more boys of different sizes came out of the huts, and called out. And Hilton said 'They seem to live very friendly.' But I wondered why the young men had paid so little attention to the boys. Why didn't they hug them and kiss them? Wouldn't they have, if they'd been Italians?

Hilton said they didn't look like real gypsies, and perhaps they didn't. But they didn't look like ordinary English country people either.

Were they really as happy as they seemed?

Mr Cornish

Kennedy[1] told me that when he was at Eton he and another boy once went for a walk, and somewhere a long way off, in a wood, they met the Vice Provost. When he came up to them he said, with his pained look, 'It's very difficult to find anything to do, isn't it?' and then went on.

---

[1] George Kennedy, the architect, who Strachey hoped would design a house for him.

ON THE BOAT. (Folkestone to Boulogne.)

The English Upper Classes were well represented. Directly I came on board I saw two youths from Eton, 17 or 18 years old, brothers, both with single eyeglasses. Their faces were like joints of mutton – so full-blooded and fleshy; I should have liked to dine off their cheeks, and their ears would each have made a very good mouthful. A casual observer might have thought they were dressed shabbily, except for a huge pair of fur motor-gloves dangled by one of them; but really everything they had on – their cloth caps, their short waterproofs, their old flannel trousers, and their old brown shoes – was impregnated with expensiveness. There was a look in their faces which showed both that they were born to command and that none of their commands would ever be of any good to anybody.

Then there was a plutocrat – was it Sir James Mackay?[2] – with four or five women in furs, for whom he took cabin after cabin, where they retired one after the other, while he himself stood firmly on deck outside in a yachting cap, looking like an old cock with his hens in the background. He was rather nice, in spite of his wealth and his second-rateness; but he had risen from the ranks, so that his niceness can't I'm afraid go to the credit of the Upper Classes.

There were two men (not connected) remarkable for their overcoats. The first was perhaps a baronet – about 35, with ginger hair and high colouring, and a blonde wife with

[2] Sir James Mackay, first Earl of Inchcape, the shipowner.

ineffectual diamond earrings, who no doubt was considered pretty. He fussed a great deal as we were getting near Boulogne, about his luggage, walking to and fro, and instructing stewards – with that queer, pointed, almost German-goose-step walk which must be the right thing when one's travelling, because James and I saw Lord Portsmouth doing it in exactly the same way, on the platform at Inverness in his tailcoat of grey flannel. But what was particularly striking about the Baronet was his very big and very thick and very brilliant ultramarine overcoat, which one had to look at as much as one could whenever he passed, so that it was only after he'd passed several times that one noticed that he was wearing spats and that his brown boots were almost incredibly polished. At the buffet at Boulogne afterwards, sitting with his wife next him and the maid opposite, he seemed to be quite frightened of the foreign language.

The second man was no doubt a Lord – tall, dark, and angular – rather like Victor Lytton; and *he* had on an immense *white* overcoat. The odd thing about both the overcoats was that they had evidently been got for effect, and yet there was only one thing about them over which any care had been taken – and that was the quality of the material. The blue one was a bad blue, and the white one was a poor white; and neither had any shape; and each was provided with the vulgar strap and button at the back that happens to be common now. But they must have cost at least £10 a piece; one could see that – and really one could see nothing more. Perhaps it is this inability to be interested in anything but the mere quality of materials that has made the English what they are. One sees it everywhere – in their substantial food with its abominable cooking, in their magnificent literature with its neglect of form, in their successful government with its disregard of principle. The Lord was wearing spats. Why is it that spats can give such an air of domination?

There were other classes and other nations represented in the boat: – Some very seasick Polish young ladies, some pedantic French youths, a young don from Oxford, and on the upper deck an Academician with a grizzled beard (or was he a

Russian Prince?) retching systematically into a basin. As I too began to feel a little sickish and as my soul began faintly to grow disembodied, all these seemed to suffer a strange diminution. But the English Upper Classes remained life-size to the end.

IO

THE WAR ACTED *as a catalyst to the writing of* Eminent Victorians. *Strachey altered his original concept of the book so that its theme became an ironic sifting of those Victorian pretensions that seemed to have led civilization into a holocaust of unparalleled magnitude.*

For those who are misled by his jokes and camp manner into believing that Strachey did not feel strongly about militarism it may be necessary to emphasize that, because of his poor health, there was no chance of his being called up after compulsory military service had been introduced in Britain. However, he objected to conscription in principle, had worked for the No Conscription Fellowship, and, after the passing of the Military Service Bill, registered as a conscientious objector. 'No doubt I have many feelings against joining the army which are not conscientious,' he wrote to his brother James (28 February 1916), 'but one of my feelings is that if I were to find myself doing clerical work in Class IVb – i.e. devoting all my working energy to helping on the war – I should be convinced that I was doing wrong the whole time; and if that isn't a conscientious objection I don't know what is . . . I'm willing to go to prison rather than do that work.'

On 7 March 1916 he appeared as a claimant for exemption before the Hampstead Advisory Committee, and read the following statement. The Committee rejected his claim.

CONSCIENTIOUS OBJECTOR

I HAVE A conscientious objection to assisting, by any deliberate action of mine, in carrying on the war. This objection is not based upon religious belief, but upon moral considerations, at which I arrived after long and careful thought. I do not wish to assert the extremely general proposition that I should never, in any circumstances, be justified in taking part in any conceivable war; to dogmatize so absolutely upon a point so abstract would appear to me to be unreasonable. At the same time, my feeling is directed not simply against the present war: I am convinced that the whole system by which it is sought to settle international disputes by force is profoundly evil; and that, so far as I am concerned, I should be doing wrong to take any active part in it.

These conclusions have crystallized in my mind since the outbreak of war. Before that time, I was principally occupied with literary and speculative matters; but, with the war, the supreme importance of international questions was forced upon my attention. My opinions in general have been for many years strongly critical of the whole structure of society; and, after a study of the diplomatic situation, and of the literature, both controversial and philosophical, arising out of the war, they developed naturally with those which I now hold. My convictions as to my duty with regard to the war have not been formed either rashly or lightly; and I shall not act against those convictions, whatever the consequences may be.

II

REJECTED AS A *conscientious objector, Strachey was also rejected as medically unfit for any kind of military service. By June 1916 he was officially a free man – for the time being. Already he had completed the first two essays of* Eminent Victorians, *'Cardinal Manning' and 'Florence Nightingale', and was half-way through 'Dr Arnold'. Through the columns of the* New Statesman, *he was campaigning for an end to barbarism and the re-introduction of civilized standards of behaviour.*

On June 26 he was staying at Wissett Lodge, a remote Suffolk farmhouse which Duncan Grant had rented from the executors of his cousin Florence Ewbank, to set himself and David Garnett up as official fruit farmers under the National Service Act. His description of this Suffolk colony of Bloomsbury gives an authentic picture of that matriarchy, presided over by Vanessa Bell, who was soon to reproduce its seductive atmosphere at Charleston farmhouse. Strachey felt its appeal very strongly – bees and blackberries, gooseberry-bushes and easels and endless arguing about art. 'Everything and everybody seems to be more or less overgrown with vegetation,' he wrote to Ottoline Morrell (20 June), 'thistles four feet high fill the flower garden, Duncan is covered with Virginia (or should it be Vanessa?) creeper, and Norton and I go about pulling up the weeds and peeping under the foliage. Norton is in very good spirits, having evolved a new theory of cubic roots.' And to Virginia Woolf he wrote: 'Is it the secret of life or of . . . something else . . . I don't quite know what? . . . Oblivion?

Stupor? Incurable looseness? – that they discovered at Wissett? I loved it, and never wanted to go away.'

To read this essay in context, one should also have read a letter Strachey wrote the previous month to Maynard Keynes: 'It is horrid to sit helpless while those poor creatures [the soldiers] are going through such things. But really one would have to be God Almighty to be of any effective use.'

MONDAY JUNE 26th 1916

TO COME CLOSE to life! To look at it, not through the eyes of Poets and Novelists, with their beautifying arrangements or their selected realisms, but simply as one actually *does* look at it, when it happens, with its minuteness and its multiplicity and its intensity, vivid and complete! To do that! To do that even with a bit of it – with no more than a single day – to realize absolutely the events of a single and not extraordinary day – surely that might be no less marvellous than a novel or even a poem, and still more illuminating, perhaps! If one *could* do it! But one can't, of course. One has neither the power nor the mere physical possibility for enchaining that almost infinite succession; one's memory is baffled; and then – the things one remembers most one cannot, one dares not – no! one can only come close to *them* in a very peculiar secrecy; and yet . . . there remains a good deal that one can and may even perhaps positively *ought* to give a fixity to, after all!

I had already had some vague, half-dreaming thoughts about the Piero della Francesca portrait downstairs, and whether what Duncan had said about the goodness of the composition was really true, & whether Norton's exclamation about both his and Nessa's[1] self-delusion . . . when I was woken up properly by Blanche putting my breakfast-tray down on the table beside me, and pulling the curtains. It was eight o'clock. I was happy – as usual – to find food before me, all ready to be eaten; I certainly wanted nothing else in the

[1] Vanessa Bell.

world just then; but, having put on my eye-glasses, I saw two letters crouching under a plate, and realized that I was very glad to have letters too. One was some damned bill, and the other was a huge affair from Ottoline; I opened it, and saw that it covered sheets and that it had enclosures, so I thought that before reading it I'll have my breakfast. And then, as I ate my boiled egg and drank my rather thick tea – but the toast was on its accustomed royal scale – I suddenly remembered the dubiousness of my position, and all that I had decided the night before. Nessa's – yes, one could only call it sulkiness – that oppressed silence all the evening after our late return – how could I doubt its meaning? – 'For heaven's sake – *can't* you leave me with Duncan for a moment? Is it *never* to be?' How her dumb animality – like some creature aux abois, as I've often thought – came out more unmistakably than I'd ever known! And yet, perhaps it *was* a mistake! How can one tell, I reflected, what that woman's thinking, with her extraordinary simplicities? But I was as certain as ever that I must do something to settle it one way or the other, that I should have to suggest my going, which meant of course Norton's too, I'd no doubt, and then – I could judge from how she took it what I was to do next. I did not like the thought of going away, though why I didn't I could not be sure. Certainly it might have been a much happier visit; somehow, I had been lonely – and why? There was Norton to talk to me about the war and mathematics – wasn't that enough to satisfy me? – And they were all very kind; but had they been kind enough? Was it their married state that oppressed me? But then – were *they* married? – Perhaps it was their *un*married state. Perhaps if I could have lain with Bunny[2] – and then I smiled to think of my romantic visions before coming – of a recrudescence of that affair, under Duncan's nose – and of his dimness on my arrival, and of how very very little I wanted to lie with him now! – Only, all the same, the thought of going away depressed me. Perhaps it was simply because of the easy-goingness of the place and the quantities of food, or was it because . . . and then

[2] David Garnett.

the vision of that young postman with the fair hair and lovely country complexion who had smiled at me and said 'Good evening, sir', as he passed on his bicycle, flashed upon me, and that other unexpected meeting – but I felt that *that* train of thought was too exciting to be hurried over, and decided, as I'd finished my breakfast, to get through Ott's letter before anything else.

I enjoyed reading it; for it was one of her tremendously expansive and affectionate letters, which invariably carry me off my feet. And it showed me (*apparently*) that she was not annoyed with me (though why one should care whether she was annoyed or not . . .) and that she was ready to have me back again at Garsington, which was a relief, because, if I *had* to go away, it was as well to have somewhere to go to. As for the enclosure, it was an appalling coloured photograph of a young man by Titian, all vague and turd-tinted, and incredibly sentimental, which I was to give to Duncan with her love.

It took a long time getting all the writing clear, but I did it at last; and then, feeling considerably more cheerful, I fished my manuscripts out of the big envelope which I'd put the night before on the lower shelf of the table and began brooding over my poem on Kisses, but I added nothing, and my digestion beginning to work, I fell back drowsily on the pillow, and for a moment there was L. before my eyes. But only for a moment; it was the post-youth who fascinated me now. My scheme of meeting him in the long lane past the village recurred to me, and then I began embroidering romantic and only *just* possible adventures which might follow – the bedroom in the inn at Norwich, and all the rest; but there was the necessity of talking to him first; and I went once more through the calculations of time and place, and saw that my plan really might, if I had the nerve, come off. The down on his cheek, the delicious down on his cheek! It was true that his nose had looked stupid, but perhaps not *too* stupid. Oh! there was no doubt that he was nice. Why, why, had Norton been with me at that second meeting? And he had not even looked in his direction! He had not even been aware that a bicycle had passed!

It was about eleven by the time I was dressed, and when I

came down I found Norton and Duncan in the drawing-room. I had hardly finished reading them Ott's letter when Vanessa came in. I gave it to her to read to herself, and of course she could hardly spell out a word of it, and thought a good deal of it dull. I was slightly annoyed, and went off to the dreadful E.C.,[3] where I could only just scrape together enough earth out of the tin coal-scuttle to cover my addition to the mountain, which, even before my addition, had been far too high.

The sun was shining, and there was my chair in the little arbour at the corner of the lawn. And Blanche came with my midday cocoa, and after that I studied the Bishop of Oxford's book on the Sermon on the Mount. It was a foolish book, but I found in it a charming little poem by an old lady in Torquay to Florrie Ewbank about the coal-strike and the neighbours and 'Sweep' who turned out to be a new dog – 'such a companion'. It was as good as anything in Samuel Butler. Then I saw that the time had come to face Vanessa. I went upstairs, and knocked at the door of her studio-room, which I'd never been in before, and went in, and there she was in front of me in the white room, on a dilapidated basket chair, and in one of her most collapsed and dreamy attitudes.

Was she plain or beautiful? I could not decide. I talked vaguely – about the room, about Ottoline – and she was very nice. I suddenly wondered why I had knocked at the door; was it idiotic? How well I know her! – And how little – how very little! Even her face, which seemed now almost chocolate-coloured, was strangely unfamiliar. If I could only have flung myself into her arms! – But I knew so well what would happen – her smile – her half-bewilderment, half infinitely sensible acceptance – and her odd relapse. As it was, I walked about uncomfortably, looking at moments vaguely out of the window; and I was decidedly uneasy when I said at last 'I think I shall have to drift off'. Of course she simply answered 'Shall you really?' I said, 'Yes – I think so – I think tomorrow.' She said 'Will you go to Garsington?' And I saw then, in the same moment, both that I couldn't bear the thought of going, and

[3] Earth Closet.

that I should have to go. I thought that perhaps she would have liked me to stay if that hadn't involved Norton's also staying; but I felt unable to disentangle that – and I got no atom of encouragement. When I had got out of the room, I entirely failed to shut the door, after repeated efforts; there was something wrong with the lock. She called out, still in her chair, that she would shut it. Before going, I had wildly glanced at a picture half-painted on an easel, representing a group of people, with what was apparently a saint in a halo in mid-air. It looked very niggly, and the colours were extremely garish – altogether it alarmed me. In the drawing-room I found the Daily News and the Daily Mirror, and went out with them into the garden again.

Norton had vanished; his chair in the sun was empty. There were only the children playing by the pond. I was terrified of their coming and pulling me to pieces, but for some reason or other they didn't, and I could read my newspapers in peace. I read the Daily News, but there was nothing to interest me. As for the Daily Mirror, what *could* there be to interest me in that? A face perhaps . . . but for weeks past I had never found a single one that wasn't disgusting; and I thought of that time at the Lacket, when every day I had found some living creature in it –usually killed. And then I *did* come on a face – a charming one – of a young boxer – 'Jimmy Wilde, the famous flyweight', whom I'd never heard of before. I longed to go and see him boxing: I have never seen a boxing-match. What would happen? I wondered. Would the blood pour down over his eyes? But the match he was to box was to be that very night, so that was impossible – though for a second I actually envisaged going up to London on some excuse that afternoon. But then – the post-boy? No! It was all ridiculous: the boxing match would come and go without me; and after that what chance would I have of ever seeing Jimmy Wilde again? At that moment I looked up, and saw, slowly pounding along the farm-road on the other side of the house, a waggon and horses, driven by a youth. It was too far off to be sure, but he seemed handsome, I was feeling désœuvré and distracted, and so I thought I'll go and see what he was like. But then I thought after all I wouldn't, and remained sitting there – undecided, vague and miserable. I was in my slippers, I reflected: and how could I go through the dirt? The cart and horses and young man had vanished; but they might still be in the farm-yard: should I go after all? I still waited. I begun to think that I should have to tell Norton that I was going next day, and that he would certainly then say that he was going too, so that we should have to travel together to London; oh! was there no way out of that? Or should I rather like it, really? He was so amusing, and so agreeable, and I liked talking to him; but how could one have adventures when he was there? Suddenly, for no apparent reason, I got up, went in, went up to my room, put on my boots, and came down again, and walked by the back way into the farm-yard.

There was no sign of a waggon; but I noticed, what I'd never noticed before, that the farm-road did not end in the farmyard, but continued past some indefinite pig-styes, through a field, and then turned round a corner out of sight. So after all the waggon – and the waggonner – might be further on – not very far away – engaged in some promiscuous occupation. I began to walk through the farmyard, when Bunny appeared, at the door of a barn.

He was in his shirt, with the sleeves rolled up, engaged also, apparently, in some extremely promiscuous occupation. What *was* he always doing in those odd purlieus? Something with the rabbits I suppose.

I talked with him – vaguely; and felt once more the pleasure of being able to do that. And the happier I felt, the more my heart sank at the thought of going away. It sank down and down, and I kept chattering with him about the hens, and wanted to take hold of his large brown bare arm. *That* I knew was beautiful; and then my heart sank so very low that I conceived the possibility of *his* asking me to stay on, if I could suggest adroitly enough that I should like to. But who can be adroit with his heart in his boots? My attempt was really feeble; and when I blurted out, apropos of nothing, that I was going tomorrow, he said, in his charming way 'Oh, I *am* sorry', and I saw that I was dished again.

Then, after a little more talking – about the new Dostoievsky – I went on along the path, and he disappeared into the recesses of the barn. I passed the indeterminate pig-styes, went through a gate, turned the corner, and found myself in a field. No waggon was anywhere in view, but, as I crossed the field, I forgot all about it – I could think of nothing but the mere pleasure and beauty of the summer day. I came into a second field, and then, to one side of me, the country dipped down at a little distance, rising again in a lovely little landscape – lovely and yet perfectly ordinary – of fields and trees and hedges and blue sky. And the field I was in was full of splendid grasses, and there were wild flowers scattered all about, and wild roses in the hedge at my left hand. I walked entranced; that feeling of a sudden explanation came upon me – a sudden easy mysterious explanation of all the long difficult mysterious embroilments of the world. 'Est-ce que j'ai trouvé le grand Peut-être?' I thought. 'Am I luckier even than Rabelais? – How miraculously lucky I am!' And I sat down, absolutely comfortable, with a little bank of earth under the hedge for my back to lean against, and the charming English prospect before my eyes. I thought of my friends, and my extraordinary happiness. I thought of Death, of Keats and the Ode to the Nightingale, of 'easeful Death' – 'half in love with easeful Death' – and I was convinced, as I'd been convinced in the train coming down from London that if Death would only come to one in a mood of serene happiness, he would be very welcome. I thought of suddenly dying, painlessly, where I lay. I wondered whether that was morbid; and then I imagined them finding my dead body – so singularly thin – and what their thoughts would be. All the time the sun warmed me deliciously, and the landscape beamed in front of me, and visions of Jimmy Wilde, half naked, with bruised ears, floated in my imagination – or dressed, in a fascinating tweed suit, rather too big for him, staying with me for a week-end at my cottage at Garsington, coming out through the door onto the lawn . . . And L? . . . The dazzling happiness, coming, in flood after flood, over my soul, was so intense that it was like a religious conversion. And through it all there was an odd waft of melancholy – a kind of vibration of regret. A strange importance seemed to invest and involve into a unity the scene, the moment, and my state of feeling. But at last I knew it was time to go back to the house. As I walked back, I felt as if I had made an advance – as if I had got somewhere new. But it seemed far shorter going back than going, and very soon I was through the back premises, and, coming onto the lawn through the gap in the bushes, found them all quite close to me sitting in the verandah, having lunch. I was late – they had almost finished their meat – and it occurred to me that all the time I had been there I had never been late for lunch before. Nessa seemed slightly surprised, and asked me whether I'd been for a long walk. My plate was filled with food, and as I ate I began to ask Duncan about the National Sporting Club – whether he had ever been there, and what boxing was like. The wretch saw at once what I was up to and said 'You've been looking at the Daily Mirror'; I didn't attempt to deny it, and went on with my questions; but his answers were unsatisfactory. He said that I would certainly enjoy the National Sporting Club very much, because one had to go there in evening dress, and that I might get Lord Henry Bentinck to take me; but he admitted that he'd never been there himself; and Nessa said that he didn't understand me at all. Bunny advised me to go to some boxing haunt in the East End that he knew of, where he said the blood flowed by the bucket-full. Norton pursed himself up, and said that all this was very disgusting, and said that I was like Nero at a gladiatorial show. I rather testily replied that he was an 'anachoret', and Nessa again took my side. Then the conversation somehow got on to George, and my relations with him, and Duncan's relations with him; and Duncan was very amusing, confessing that he still sometimes thought of him sentimentally, and that at one time he would have been willing to give him a hundred a year, to have him as his mistress. We asked him where he would have got a hundred a year from, to give to George. He said he would have borrowed it. We asked 'Who from?' And Norton and I at once saw that of course it would have been from Maynard, and everybody laughed. After that Ottoline loomed up in her accustomed style, and there was a long and rather fierce argument as to whether she had any artistic capacity, and whether she was 'creative'; I said that she was, and that Garsington proved it; but all the others were against me. Norton declared that Garsington was the work of a bower-bird, and that to talk of its showing 'creativeness' was absurd. I answered in a voice more contemptuous than my feeling but gradually I felt my feeling growing as contemptuous as my voice. Then Nessa began on the 'artistic' tack, and for a moment I almost became better; all that violent discussion of my second evening shimmered in the background, and I got as far as saying that I didn't think I agreed with her notion of art. But it passed off, and the children appeared, and we all got up from the table. I found myself standing next to Duncan on the lawn, and he was holding the Daily Mirror open at the picture of Jimmy Wilde. I said 'Don't you think he's beautiful?' And he said 'Yes'; but added almost immediately, 'I expect it's only because he hasn't got a collar on. If his neck was covered he's probably look like anyone else.' I didn't believe it, and I was slightly annoyed.

Then I went upstairs, heavy with all that eating, and lay down on my bed, where I began again thinking out my plan of campaign with the postboy, until I fell asleep; and I slept solidly for over an hour. I was woken up by the piercing screams of the children, as they played on the little piece of grass outside my window. The noise gradually penetrated my sleep, and reached a climax with Quentin bursting into sobs. I heard Julian's[4] cockney voice, full of guilt and self-justification, calling out to Flossie ('Flossay') that Quentin was very naughty and would *not* play with him. After a confused interval, Nessa's voice emerged – low and plaintive – 'I've *told* you, Julian, that you must *not* . . . You're much stronger than Quentin, and he can't defend himself . . . I've *told* you . . .' And then utter silence on the part of Julian. Irritation came upon me at the woman's weakness. – Or *was* it weakness? Wasn't it perhaps simply common sense? Did she see that no amount of punishment would ever prevent Julian from being

[4] Julian Bell, the eldest son of Clive and Vanessa Bell, was then eight years old.

cruel? That it would only make him dislike her to no purpose? Perhaps; but still I was angry with her for her lack of indignation; and my hatred of Julian was intense.

However, silence was re-established, and I picked up the copy of Temple Bar on the bed-table, to see if there was anything in it that I hadn't already read. I struck at once upon an article by some woman or other on political parties in Bohemia. It was all entirely new to me, and most interesting; I had never before seen the names of Rieger or Gregr; I knew nothing whatever of the history of those movements. The article was not very profound, but it was not badly done either. I was amazed and appalled by my ignorance – that at the age of 36 it should only be by a chance article in a back number of a second-rate magazine, written by an unknown woman, that I should have become acquainted with facts of that magnitude, with names as important in Austrian history as those of O'Connell and Parnell in ours. And I, and my likes, are supposed to be well educated persons! I then skimmed an article on Thurlow, which was slightly interesting too; by that time it was four o'clock, and I got up and went downstairs for my afternoon stroll.

On the lawn I saw Norton reading mathematics so I took the opportunity of telling him that I had decided to go away next day; and he immediately announced that he would go with me. I assented, and drifted off, leaving him with his mathematics.

I drifted down the dreary road that goes in the opposite direction to the village. My mind, which (with exception of the interval of sleep) had been in a state of constant activity since 8 o'clock in the morning, now relapsed into dreaminess. The expectation of tea was one of the few things definitely present to it, as I walked along between the hedges on the empty road. – That, and the feeling that it was only *after* tea that anything exciting could happen – that *then* something exciting would happen – that *then* there would be the crisis of the meeting with the bicycle, and the conversation, and all the possibilities involved – so that *until* then I had nothing to do but to meander about and fill up the interval as best I could. I fancy I thought a little about Sarah Bernhardt, and, after I'd turned back, the puzzle of my relations with women flickered before me. Carrington[5] occurred to me, and then, for some odd reason, Maria.[6] Why on earth had I been so chaste during those Latin lessons? I saw how easily I could have been otherwise – how I might have put my hand on her bare neck, and even up her legs, with considerable enjoyment; and probably she would have been on the whole rather pleased. I became certain that the solution was that I was restrained by my knowledge that she would certainly inform 'Auntie'[7] of every detail of what had happened, at the earliest possible opportunity. It would be practically copulating with Ott looking through the keyhole – which I was by no means prepared to do. There are limits in these matters, I reflected; strange that it should be so, but there are. I turned in at the gate, passed the angle of the house, and saw to my delight that tea was ready and Vanessa actually pouring it out.

Norton appeared immediately, and Duncan and Bunny a little later. There was not very much conversation; what there was chiefly circled round the question of the train that Norton and I should go by. He wanted to go after lunch, and I wanted to go after tea. As he had no motive to produce and I had – viz. that dinner in a train was so amusing – it was eventually settled that I should have my way. I ate my frugal spongefingers contentedly, listening to their gibes. Duncan at last got up and went into the drawing-room, where he began to play his Bach composition. I followed him, with what I hoped was an air of detachment, pretended to look for a book, went out through the drawing-room door into the passage, and so through the front door out of the house.

My fear had been that Norton would want to walk out with me, but I seemed to have escaped him successfully. He would hardly follow me now. The time, too, was exactly right, so far as I could judge. I had nothing to do now but to walk forward,

[5] Strachey had met the painter Dora Carrington the previous autumn, and she had fallen in love with him.
[6] Maria Nys, who later became the first wife of Aldous Huxley.
[7] Lady Ottoline Morrell.

and I was bound to meet . . . the bicycle, either before I got to the pillar-box at the crossroads, or, if necessary, *at* it. I walked down the road towards the village, wondering how it would turn out. I felt to see that I had my letter to Ottoline in my pocket, and rehearsed the meeting – my stopping him, my asking him if he would mind taking the letter, and then, somehow, my offering him a cigarette. It was fairly clear, although I foresaw that the actual stopping of the bicycle might be difficult – especially if he was coming down hill – so far it was fairly clear; but after the opening – *after* the preliminary conversation and the cigarette – then everything was a blank, to be filled in at the moment according to his amiability, and as my presence of mind would suggest. But both his amiability and my presence of mind were highly dubious entities. I had the wildest, and the bleakest, visions – of amusement and charm and successes culminating in Norwich, and of crushing failure – sheer stupidity, or un-disguised annoyance – or perhaps of missing him altogether by some unforeseen mischance. It was a preposterous errand! I laughed, and imagined myself reading about myself in a novel by Tolstoy – reading quickly, and turning over the pages as fast as I could, in my excitement to know what would happen in the end. What *would* happen? I took the shortcut by the field with the poppies, emerged onto the high road, turned to the left, away from the village, and then off to the right, up the long narrow lane, at the end of which was the pillar-box. It was half-past five; the collection at the pillar-box was due at five minutes to six; the lane was probably about two miles long; therefore, if he was punctual, it seemed certain that I should meet him in it, as there was no other way from the pillar-box to the village, and he had to be in the village at half-past six. I had remembered the lane as being fairly level, but now it seemed to go up and down in the most alarming manner. If I were to come upon him as he was on a downward dip – should I have the nerve – or even the strength of voice – to stop him? And wouldn't he be furious if I did? Perhaps he would be mollified if he saw that my letter was to a Ladyship. Or perhaps . . . my mind lost itself in speculations. I imagined his nose, his cheek,

and his complexion with a tantalizing mixture of indistinct-
ness and intensity. His cap, too, and his yellow hair, lighter
than his skin – and that odd armlet . . . and why, to be sure,
wasn't he in the army? Surely he wasn't under age? . . . A
woman in a drab mackintosh appeared on the road in front of
me, going in the same direction. I passed her easily, and sped
on. It seemed almost probably that I should reach the pillar-
box before he did, in which case I should have to linger about;
and then – if there were other people there? – old gaffers
posting letters to their sons at the front? I might be done for in
that case. I had passed the turning down which Norton and I
had gone after meeting him the time before, so that, supposing
the time to have been the same on that occasion, he might
appear at any moment now. But he didn't appear: the lane
went on and on indefinitely, its only merit being that it kept
more or less straight, so that one could see people approaching
from a good distance, and prepare accordingly. But no one did
approach. Meanwhile the sky had been growing darker and
darker, and I expected it to rain at any moment; that would be
an additional complication. Then I saw that the pillar-box
could not be far off; it was almost in sight, in a group of trees in
front of me. I had no doubt; I recognized the place from some
cottages on the right hand, so I *should* have to wait there, after
all. Suddenly I heard a whistle – and an immediate remi-
niscence flashed upon me: it was of 'Signor Grasso', the
postman on the Loch-an-Eilan road, when he came on his
bicycle with the letters in the morning. My mind shot back for
an instant to Milton Cottage – how many years ago? – with
Pippa and Pernel in the garden, and Sharp Cottage, too, and its
dreariness, and James of course – it all came and went in a
moment; was it possible that *he* too—? That he was whistling
to warn those cottages that he was coming? Oh no! Such things
weren't done out of the Highlands . . . and then his bicycle
appeared, slowly advancing: it *was* he, there could be no
doubt. But he did not stop at the cottage, he came on, and we
should meet almost at once. He looked rather bigger than I
remembered him, and he had something in his mouth – a
cigarette? Then *that* plan was shattered. But I saw at once that

it was the whistle, and as I took the letter out of my pocket he actually began slowing down, almost as if he was expecting me to give it him. 'This is a very favourable beginning', I thought. And on the very heels of that, came the perception that something was all wrong, hopelessly wrong, that he wasn't – that he couldn't be – that it was somebody else. Yes, it was another postman, with black hair, and a red Presbyterian face, and a most unattractive briskness about him altogether, stopping with an écœurant politeness to take my letter, as I handed it to him, saying 'Would you mind taking this?' with the most natural air in the world. 'So *that's* all over,' I said to myself, as he vanished, and I turned automatically on my tracks, for obviously there was now nothing to be done but to trudge back home. I nearly burst out laughing aloud at the farcicality of my proceedings, but was restrained by the re-appearance of the woman in the mackintosh, whom I now saw, as I passed her, looked like a lower-class Vernon Lee. I began to wonder what had happened – why he had failed me – whether it was only a temporary change, or whether . . . Perhaps he'd joined the army, perhaps that armlet meant that he was going to be called up, and very likely, as today was Monday . . . anyhow it was just like my luck. There was a servant-maid waiting at the corner of the branch road – waiting rather mysteriously; she was pretty, and sad. Could she have been waiting for. . . ? I passed on, and by this time the clouds had disappeared from the sky and the sun was out again. I thought of the youth at Lockeridge who had been obliterated in the same silent way: but, after all, I considered, some remain. There are so many possibilities in this world, and I shouldn't have been much surprised if something extra-ordinary had happened almost at once. But nothing happened, except that, quite suddenly and apparently irrelevantly, a phrase from Handel sounded in my mind – a phrase that I don't believe I'd thought of for years. – 'Rejoice! Rejoice! Rejoi-oi-oi-oi-oice greatly!' And then the thought occurred to me of writing this microscopic description of a day. I was delighted with the idea, and went on elaborating it for a long time, until at last I drifted into the plan of a satirical poem on

Winston in the style of the chorusses in Samson Agonistes, which should begin

> 'Strange are the ways of men;
> And the ways of God are still more curious;'

and I was still murmuring these lines when I reached the house; and as I went upstairs to my room I saw that they would have to end the poem too.

In my room, I fell with extraordinary energy on my Arabian story, which I had a wild notion that I might finish before dinner. It was obvious, really, that I couldn't, yet I wrote on at top speed for more than an hour, covering the pages in a most unusual manner. I heard them calling to me to come to dinner, but still wrote. They called again, and then I realized that it was useless going on – the wretched thing wasn't nearly finished; so I went down into the kitchen and had dinner with them – rather silent, while they discussed the superfetation of rabbits, and whether wildflowers might be legitimately classified as yellow, blue and red.

I went out of the room before anyone else, and walked through the drawing-room out onto the lawn. It was still quite light, though it must have been past nine o'clock. I paced once or twice up and down the lawn, when Bunny appeared and immediately joined me. I had a sharp and most queer feeling that it was somehow done by arrangement – though of course we had arranged nothing of the sort. We went at once through the pergola into the strip of kitchen garden, and began walking up and down the path. I felt nervous, almost neurasthenic – what used to be called 'unstrung'. He was so calm and gentle, and his body was so large, with his shirt (with nothing under it) open all the way down – that I longed to throw myself onto him as if he were a feather-bed, to tell him everything – everything, and to sob myself asleep. And yet, at the same time, the more I longed to expand, the more I hated the thought of it. It would be disgusting and ridiculous – it was out of the question. And I became astringent, and would talk of nothing but the vegetables as we walked up and down. The vegetables, and still the vegetables – it almost seemed at last that there was nothing else that one could possibly talk about; and, as the subject was not very interesting, why not give it up and go in? I was in terror that this would happen, and yet my congealment was such that when, at the end of one of our turns, we got to the pergola, I made as if to go through it, back on to the lawn. At that, he came out in that lovely firm way that he sometimes so unexpectedly has, and turned right off through an aspara- gus bed into that other more remote part of the garden, where the grass is so thick and lush, and everything is tangled and overgrown with weeds and roses – a place that trembles on the edge of sentimentality, but is saved by being so small and unkempt and tumbledown. We went and sat on a dirty wooden seat at the farthest end of it, and I thought that if it had been a clean stone seat, and if he had been dressed in white knee-breeches and a blue coat with brass buttons, and if I had been a young lady in a high waist – or should it have been the other way round? – the scene would have done very well for an Academy picture by Marcus Stone.

And so we did talk at last – about other things than vegetables – about Barbara,[8] and that fandango of the letter; and he made me realize what a charming creature she was. And he chaffed me about my 'affair with Carrington',[9] and I explained in great detail that it couldn't be called that; and as we talked I grew comfortable, and in fact happy; and then, when the conversation touched upon the changeability of moods, I said that I had been in a wretched mood all day, that I had felt everything with an unnatural acuteness, as if I had had

[8] Barbara Hiles, an ex-Slade student and friend of Carrington's, who married Nicholas Bagenal.

[9] 'What I remember must have been the next day – the day he apparently left', David Garnett told the editor. 'We went for a walk along the edge of a cornfield and he told me that he was in love, or more than a little in love with Carrington and made me promise not to tell Vanessa or Duncan or anyone. He was afraid of Ottoline finding out – and I think of Virginia also. I kept my promise . . . I suppose it was the reassurance I had given him which led him to confide in me and he was also perhaps more ready to confide a hetero-sexual attachment to me than a daydream about the postman which would have strained my powers of sympathy!'

no skin. It wasn't at all an accurate statement, and his sympathy – 'Oh Lytton, how dreadful!' – made me feel myself a silly beast, and I quickly covered my tracks by bringing up the subject of his life at Wissett, and his prospects, and his general state. He talked for a long time about these things – about his settled happiness and the problems of his future – and I felt very sympathetic, and wished I had several thousand a year. He was amusing, too, very amusing, and I saw how shy and distrustful of himself he was in company. It grew darker and colder, but we stayed on. At last it seemed quite natural to ask him whether he thought they really liked me. 'Who, Lytton?' –'Duncan and Vanessa – no, not really; but sometimes they seem very severe. Perhaps I'm too uppish'. 'Oh Lytton, how absurd you are. They call you "the old gentleman". I heard them saying that they hoped the old gentleman was happy.' – The darling! How beautifully he had smoothed me down! So that everything was now calm and good – so that that was the ordinary state of the world – and all those doubts and itches – how futile and preposterous! I laughed, and said 'Do *you* call me "the old gentleman?" ' He answered, flirting, 'The Prince of Darkness is a gentleman'. Without any difficulty I stretched out my hand and put it into his breast, which was glowing a warm pink in the twilight. I said 'An *old* gentleman?' and he answered 'No; that's just the difference'. 'Have I more experience than the Devil?' I murmured as we laughed. We came nearer to one another, and, with a divine vigour, embraced. I was amused to notice, just before it happened, that he looked very nervously in the direction of the house. We kissed a great deal, and I was happy. Physically, as well as mentally, he had assuaged me. That was what was so wonderful about him – he gave neither too little nor too much. I felt neither the disillusionment of having gone too far, nor any of the impatience of desire. I knew that we loved each other, and I was unaware that my cock had moved.

It was too cold to stay out any longer, and we came in to find the room in almost pitch darkness, with three figures over the fire. He went out with Duncan; left alone with Norton and Nessa, I instantly realised that we must have been out rather a long time. Norton said something which I took for an indecent joke, and I answered with unnecessary self-consciousness; then, of course, he said that he had meant nothing at all. There was a long pause, during which I imagined Duncan furious in the kitchen, and Bunny pacifying him. But when they appeared at last with the lamp, Duncan seemed perfectly cheerful, and the evening at once became very gay. We ranged over Ka[10] and her complicated history, we discussed our private weaknesses, and ended in a fantastic [blank in MS] of idiotic rhymes.

'Ka is my Ma,
But who is my Pa?'

was Norton's first inspiration, which set us all off in a string. How adorable was Nessa, as she sat, rocking with laughter at the bawdiness of the jokes! We got up from our chairs somehow, at about one o'clock. Duncan and Bunny disappeared as usual, to lock up. Nessa went off, and Norton briskly mounted his attic-ladder. I tore off my clothes in my bedroom, with only one desire – to sleep. In bed, I thought of Bunny, and then, as I was dozing off, something strange happened. I suddenly found myself with Duncan under the bushes in the drizzle on that first afternoon on Hampstead Heath. The vividness of it was so great that I woke up with a start. Then that too melted in oblivion; and it was L who was with me when I finally fell asleep.

[10] Katherine Cox, the robust Fabian with whom Rupert Brooke had been in love, and who afterwards married Will Arnold-Forster.

12

BY THE END of 1917 Strachey had set up house at Tidmarsh, near Pangbourne, with Dora Carrington, the ex-Slade student who devoted the last sixteen years of her life to him. The following year *Eminent Victorians was published. Its impact was tremendous. The world was weary of big guns and phrases, and Strachey's polemic was especially appealing to the younger generation. Later this year he met Ralph Partridge, a burly blue-eyed rowing blue from Oxford, who had distinguished himself in the trenches, rising to the rank of major while still in his early twenties. This was the beginning of a curious tri-liaison: Strachey became infatuated with Partridge, who wished to marry Carrington, who was deeply in love with Strachey. In the spring of 1919, Partridge and Carrington went off on an experimental holiday together in Spain, returning to England early in May.*

Strachey's 'agitation and happiness' some time later that month (his dating is bizarre) may, or possibly may not, refer to Partridge. What is interesting is to see that, however much his life and circumstances had changed since Leamington College, the nature of his homosexual intrigues remained pretty well the same.

MAY 17th – MAY 15th 1919

Savile Club,
107 Piccadilly, W.

Agitation and happiness. The future so important: if – The delicious past. A fairy story? The little plot, the gay room, the accueil; the servants incidentally. Being left en tête-à-tête. Galeotto fa il libre! The undress – the motor drive. Strength and kindness. Ah! Mon dieu! The semi-assignations.

Folly? Not to have been more definite? to have clinched it? Or wisdom to wait?

The sense of decision – overpowering. The possibilities. If – . . . The dream-like-ness of everything, the recklessness about ordinary cares. So heavenly to have such an end in view! Sensitiveness combined with aloofness. And then the suitability of Spring.

Longings to rush away, and cover one's head with one's hands – burst into tears perhaps. Thoughts that fill every moment. Amusement, too – at the absurdity and the secrecy. The secrecy vital, and yet the mad desire to tell. Has anyone ever experienced such romantic moments? – such intensities of curious delight? It's difficult to believe it. The bizarrerie and the excitement; the contradictions. Among the rest, certain details. Inexprimable.

13

'A FORTNIGHT IN France' was the last considerable piece of writing Strachey completed before his death. His famous biographies had all been published. From the anarchism of Eminent Victorians he had reverted to his natural romanticism and produced in Queen Victoria (1921) a perfectly constructed Life that playfully enhanced the legend of the little old lady on the throne. In 1928 came his last major biography, Elizabeth and Essex, a tapestry depicting scenes of theatrical drama, between the lines of which may be read something of his own relationship with the handsome young Old Etonian, Roger Senhouse.

At the centre of his emotional life during these years had been a ménage-à-trois with Carrington and her husband Ralph Partridge. Round this 'Triangular Trinity of Happiness' crowded numerous men and women with parts to play in this Bloomsburgian comedy of love, and who contributed to its final tragedy.

In May 1931 Portraits in Miniature was published, and not long afterwards Strachey began his long essay on Othello (later published in its unfinished form in Characters and Commentaries and in Literary Essays). But he was already suffering from the stomach cancer that was shortly to kill him and from a feeling of disillusionment arising out of his love-affair with Roger Senhouse. Tired of emotional complexity, of 'ordinary life', he wanted to cut himself adrift from people, at least for a time. Only solitude, he felt, could relieve his weariness – solitude, plenty of comfort, good food and travel from one place to another.

He set out alone for France on 3 September 1931. As his diary shows, the two weeks of travelling did help to renew his interest in life. But within six weeks of his return home, he had taken to his bed for the last time. He died on 21 January 1932, after two months of medically supervised struggle. 'If this is dying,' he remarked, 'then I don't think much of it.'

Seven weeks later, on 11 March, wearing Strachey's yellow-silk dressing-gown, Carrington shot herself and died at Ham Spray House, where he had died.

A FORTNIGHT IN FRANCE

September 3rd, 1931. 10 p.m.

Hotel Berkeley, 7 Avenue Matignon, Paris.

Well, now that I have actually done it – gone away, if only for a minute or two & have reached this first stage of my rather preposterous journey – the result of course is far more mixed than anything else. At the present moment, satisfaction predominates. After the decidedly dreary and by no means cheap dinner at the restaurant here, I struggled out to a glass of coffee at the Rond Point – but oh, so indoors! – and then, not very conscious, strolled down the Champs Elysées towards the Place de la Concorde, in the darkness. Lights in the distance caught my eye, and then I remembered the new illuminations. I went on, beginning to be excited, and soon came to the really magical scene; the enormous Place – the surrounding statues – the twin palaces on the North side – and in the middle the astonishing spectacle of the obelisk, a brilliant luminous white, with black hieroglyphics, clear as if drawn by ink, all over it. A move to the right revealed the Madeleine; and then, looking back, I saw the Arc de Triomphe, brightly lighted, with the avenue of lamps leading to it. A most exhilarating affair! It was warm, the innumerable motors buzzed, the strollers were many and – so it seemed – sympathetic. How difficult not to revert to R![1] Of course, impossible. Partly perhaps the absurd reason of being now in the same country, but more the associations – his love of Paris – and then the odd recollec-

[1] Roger Senhouse.

tions: the Ritz bar on the way to Rome – how many years ago? – with the sinister and fascinating figure of I.C.[2] – dinner at Montagnié's (not a success) – the walk by the river, and then somehow the Gare de Lyon and that idyllic journey; useless to reflect upon now! – And that very odd Norman Douglas weekend – the double bedroom at Foyot's – my exhaustion – his coming in late at night after an evening on the prowl with N.D. – the morning excitements – ah well! ah well! And his never referring to any of it again – was I very tiresome, I wonder? – or did it just, as usual, simply never occur to him that I should like to know that he's enjoyed it? . . . But really these reflections are quite useless – and worse. At this moment no doubt he's engulfed by Bill Burton in that grotesque villa we know of with the imitation cobwebs and El Greco's – And I can be happy in my solitude.

After the last few weeks of strangely febrile imaginations, I can take a long breath – rest on my oars – look round. The unexpected climax and more unexpected failure of A.S.[3] was only one section of the excitement. The odd, very odd, recrudescence – from almost nothing – of G.H.[4] – a kind of muffled prelude – that was enthralling too. The other intense evocations – but they perhaps are hardly yet over. More than once my visionary existence has seemed more real than reality – a state of affairs that should not last too long, and the obelisk of the Place de la Concorde came as a salutary something to my mind. Typical of my condition that the T.[5] circumstance positively passed almost unnoticed in the middle of the other vagaries – a peppermint drop absentmindedly swallowed

[2] Ian Campbell.

[3] Alan Searle a friend of Somerset Maugham and later his secretary.

[4] George Harvey (1905–69) was a solicitor to whom Strachey had been introduced by Robert Gathorne-Hardy at his house near Reading. When he was leaving Strachey caressed him on the neck and said: 'You must come and visit us: we have a gibbet on the hill.' Shortly afterwards he invited Harvey to act as chauffeur on his 'little tour' of France: 'I've got a Sunbeam car, but can't drive . . . of course you would have no expenses of any kind.' Unfortunately Harvey was unable to leave his office.

[4] Probably Stephen Tomlin, the sculptor, who married Strachey's niece, the novelist Julia Strachey.

whole. But I am sleepy after the journey and the excitements of Paris – after the hideous examination of so many horrid people – after the doubts and alarms which will even still attack me about my luggage and the non-appearance of porters – after that enormous lunch in the train – after several chapters of Lord Salisbury – after the Lord knows what besides. The sudden reappearance on the boat of the very young and marvellously handsome German who travelled in the same carriage with me from Paddington to Reading a week or two ago might be mentioned – and elaborated, if I were not too sleepy, and he hadn't been so hopelessly involved with an American married female and if – But I must go to bed. Where shall I be tomorrow at 11 p.m.?

September 4th. The answer turns out to be Reims – though till the middle of lunch I thought it would be Meaux. But this ridiculous weather after relaxing for a few hours in Paris, relapsed so completely that it became obvious that Meaux would never do – so I decided hurriedly to press on here – went back to the Berkeley, packed quickly, and then owing to the vile vagueness of the dame du comtoir, nearly arrived too late at the Gare de l'Est. However, all was well; after taking my ticket I had three minutes – strolled down the immense platform to my train – only to be told by my kind porter that I'd left 'ma petite valise' behind me. It was really very clever of him to spot it – I'd put it down at the ticket guichet, and had to run like a hare for it – quite half a mile it seemed as I positively pegged along – but there it was – I seized it, pegged back and reached the train at last breathless and sweating by every pore. Not at all like a milord anglais! We passed Meaux – and I was certainly right; – no place for a wet evening, but delightful, I guessed, for wandering down pointless streets in sunshine. And so, after about two hours, Reims was reached, the rain still pouring.

It was at Foyot's, dear old Foyot's, that I had lunch, and decided to come here. This had been preceded by a stroll – a heavenly stroll – down the Rue St Honoré, where every window seemed to present something I longed for – chairs, prints, books, earrings. But I bought nothing, though I hovered for twenty minutes in Block's shop. Then the rain, and a taxi to the Louvre. Admission 2 francs – rather a disgrace to the French nation. The pictures seemed even darker than usual. I peered a little, but soon came away. Some portraits – a Condottiere – were people really like that in the 15th Century? I suppose they may have been – fierce, beautiful, and absolutely solid. But now one only meets, in that line, whited sepulchres.

Foyot's was very much as usual, with its garçonnaille, if there is such a word: – silent, gentle, cynical, faintly dramatic. What can it mean? Their short black alpaca coats, their infinitely discreet buttocks swathed in infinitely long white napkins, filled me, as usual, with speculations. The food was poor; but otherwise everything was so attractive that I almost determined to stay there, at the hotel, on the way back.

And Reims? A godforsaken city. So, at least, I decided in the drizzle on my first tour of inspection. Naturally with the cathedral bashed God goes, but what's more serious is that nearly everything else has gone as well. I had imagined a few neat German bombs had blown up the sacred building and that that was all. Far from it – the whole town was wrecked. A patched-up remnant is all that remains – the patches dated 1920. Miserable! Or so, at any rate, it appeared in the drizzle. The hotel, large, modern, and empty, was not encouraging. But, with dinner, Fortune turned her wheel. The hotel restaurant turned out to be almost impressive. A great many people too – an English family, primness incarnate, belonging to the '80's – some Germans, and so on, and the meal, including some charming champagne, was excellent. At this rate, things won't be so bad, even if the rain continues. I shall eat and drink for three days – why not? Expensive, no doubt, but I intended to be expensive; and the bed is soft, and there's a bath attached to my bedroom, and also the Brasserie de Strasbourg is attractive as an after-dinner resort for coffee. Replete and vague, I found a seat there – a leather seat against the wall – while some mechanical instrument produced songs by a baritone, and sous-off's played French billiards. A place to dream in, decidedly. My thoughts wandered to Lady Bess-borough – Lord Granville – that old tragedy – the hopeless Adonis between the two women, aunt and niece. Ah well! I suppose that divine creature got something out of it; but it's typical of the world that it should have been the lesser being – the admirable, respectable, but after all ordinary Lady Granville – who got all that she wanted. Lady Bessborough is thrilling, tragic, extremely distinguished – and who has heard of her?

The lift boy was gay on the way back to my bedroom here – six floors up. Nobody to talk to. But that's the whole point, I know; and how absurd to imagine that we might meet R in the Louvre – with Victor Butler, presumably! – and to wonder what one would say to him. Postcards to T and to C.[5] Impossible to talk of the solid foundations – it's the shiftings and difficulties that demand descriptions. My adored C, and the other R,[6] my beloved and perfect R[7] – one says nothing of them – for all is known!

September 5th. It seems almost impossible that it was only the day before yesterday that I said good-bye to C. at Victoria. Weeks appear to have elapsed – though after all really very little has happened, movement and oddity – that's all; and, owing to solitude, a curious intensification of the details of consciousness. I only wish I could describe my mental states more accurately, but their multitude and complication are far too great. Among them, so far, boredom seems not to figure; though really this ghastly weather is enough to lead to suicide. At the present moment the rain dashes against the window, as I lie on my large bed under a scarlet eiderdown. It has pelted on and off all day; the inhabitants are in despair; the vines hopeless; and the sullen sky shows no hint of changing. What a curse! As I explored the town with overcoat and umbrella this morning I tried to imagine what the bombardment could have been like – but quite failed. The unreality of war makes it a

5 Carrington.
6 Ralph Partridge.
7 Roger Senhouse.

wretched subject to think about. The Cathedral, what with pre-war restorations, war destructions, and post-war restorations, presents a deplorable spectacle. I doubt whether even in its palmiest days it was anything very much – except, probably, for the glass. I tottered away from it to lose myself in dreary streets, jumping sky-high at one moment before the startled gaze of an elderly inhabitant – an attack of the Strachey twist.

I forgot to mention an incident in the Rue St Honoré yesterday. Looking at myself in a shop-window mirror I saw for the first time how completely gray my hair was over my temples. So that has come at last! I was beginning to think it never would. Do I feel like it? Perhaps I do a little – a very little. A certain sense of detachment declares itself amid the agitations that continue to strew my path.

At any rate, thank heaven, I have achieved some kind of detachment about R. I hardly feel as if I *could* now be shattered by him as I was during the 'black period' or even during the original Burton affair two years ago. No! I am really calm – that dreadful abysmal sensation in the pit of the stomach is absent. What a relief! Whether this means that I am out of love or not I can't pretend to say. I hope it means that my feelings are at least more rational. The inexpressible charm of his presence, the sweetness of his temper, his beautiful affectionateness – why should these things make it difficult for me to accept the facts that he must be allowed to have his own tastes, and that his tastes happen not to be what I would have wished?

Lord Salisbury's Life – I read it with amazement. So singularly far from every experience of one's own. Medieval in its remoteness. These extraordinary men of action, so certain, so unreflective, so untemperamental – what is one to think of them? – 'Loyalty to the Sovereign was with him more than a sentiment.' So writes the excellent Lady Gwendolen. 'He would have placed it upon the same level of obligation as patriotism. (Good heavens, Lady Gwendolen!) His reason corroborated what his instincts impelled him to. (Indeed!) He believed the monarchy to be indispensable to the Empire', etc.

etc. Where are we? And Lord Salisbury was not only an extremely successful, but an exceedingly able man. 'Great', in fact. A line of Burns has been floating in my head as I've been reading. I don't know why – except for its utter incongruity. 'Laddie, lie near me!' Were Burns and Lord Salisbury both human beings? As for Lady Salisbury, she presumably must have occasionally experienced some such sentiment, though no doubt she could have expressed it otherwise. For the rest, an infuriating stupid woman. She complained once of the friends who would worry her by wanting to know upon what 'system' she trained her children . . . She had got no system, she said. She taught her children to say their prayers and come to the Holy Communion. That was all. 'It is not I who train them, but God the Holy Ghost!' – Laddie, lie near me! The words act as a kind of incantation, dispelling the folly of the virtuous and the hardness of the wise. Laddie, lie near me! So I ejaculate – though I am all too doubtful of the connotation; my mind is interrogative, my heart is either too full or too empty, as I murmur the lovely shibboleth, and fall asleep.

Sunday, Sept. 6th. The Brasserie de Strasbourg was at its height tonight – crammed full – waiters tearing hither and thither – and a trio – violin, 'cello and piano – supplying the music. But humanity seemed not quite equal to the occasion – ugly, foolish, dull – my waiter was too like Nigel Playfair – so I slipped away in the middle of some terrible 'selection' from Madame Butterfly. If dying were like that – leaving a party, as people say – but it all depends on what party. If one's in love with life, to leave it will be as terrible as the dreadful moment when one has to leave one's beloved one – an agony, long foreseen – almost impossibly fearful – and yet it inevitably comes. And really it is a kind of death whenever the beloved object goes; which is why sleeping together is such a peculiar solace – death is avoided –one loses consciousness deliciously alive. A head on a pillow! . . . G.B.'s[8] for instance? – A surprising occurrence – romantic – excessive; but thank

---

[8] George Bergen, the young American-Russian artist.

goodness nothing more. It would be most unpleasant to be in love with G.B.. I am sorry for Duncan—, though, after all, he doesn't seem to suffer a bit!—

My last day in Reims was positively illumined by a little sunshine. Tea on the pavement, after having inspected the Musée, with its remarkable tapestries from the cathedral and its multitude of odds and ends. As Sunday is a free day, it was full of people – why? Impossible to discover. Is it snobbery or sex that drives human beings to look at works of art, for which, in reality they care nothing at all? A pathetic business – and also a paradoxical one. The aesthetic instinct – such an intimate rarity – and making such a tremendous to-do!

The Musée, anyhow, was better than Mumm's cellars, with their pointless miles of bottles, heaven knows how many kilometres underground. In the middle of the endless avenues, about half a dozen slaves – sweet creatures – sat bottling and corking the wine. Impossible to speak to them, as the odious cripple who was showing me round gave no possible opportunity to any such thing. All I could do, as I vanished down one of the avenues, was to wave my hand to them – and I'm glad to say they waved back.

And my last night in Reims ended rather tipsily – after vague movements from café to café, the absorption of various wines, cointreau, etc. – all among this concentrated French population, occupied completely with women and money and nothing else. Sensible people! No half lights for them! No seeing round the corner, no dodgings of the issue, no self-contradicting homosexual preoccupations. Oh no! Forward, onward! In a straight line. The unfortunate English – it seems strange that they should ever have had the reputation of being practical and having common sense. It may have been so once – Lord Salisbury? – but now they have developed a positive mania for being off the point – they cannot for the life of them look a fact in the face. And their own faces betray them. One has only to see them among the French – their shapeless features, their desiccated self-conscious expressions, their idiotic little clipped moustaches – but enough! – No doubt the French are just as bad too, in their own way.

The quiet, white-haired, rather indigent Englishman at the second-rate restaurant this evening was a good example of the race. A schoolmaster perhaps – no, a cashier – with an unfortunate wife. Quiet, dim, but able to speak to the waiter with complete efficiency: I envied him; except that he had made that fatal mistake of a wife. How does one speak to waiters? One of the main problems of existence, I sometimes think. T, I believe, has some theory about it – but I'm sure it's unsound. I hate waiters, and perhaps that's why I can't speak to them. But if I loved them would it be any better?

I am beginning to drivel. To-morrow – Nancy! Hurrah!

Sept. 7th. Grand Hotel, Nancy. The hurrah is re-echoed – rather faintly – now that I've got there. Naturally enough, Reims, for the first time, was lit by the sun when I left it this morning, and as my journey went on the sun grew fainter and fainter, until at its end there was none at all. Otherwise all was easy. At Châlons, where there was about an hour to wait, I found a pleasant taxi-youth who drove me to the Cathedral. He insisted on accompanying me inside, told me he was twenty-three, not married, and explained exactly why Châlons Cathedral was inferior to Reims Cathedral. Said he'd like to come to London. Perhaps it was idiotic of me not to have stayed at Châlons for the night; he might have found me an agreeable bedroom. But the force of the pre-arranged plan was too great, and on I came, passing through flood after flood – hardly any country visible –nothing but fields of water with a few faint trees poking their heads out of them – a dismal sight! And now, in this elegant town of good King Stanislas, how can the gildings and the vistas and the twirligigs do justice to themselves without a single gleam of sunlight to set them off? My heart shows a slight tendency to sink. The hotel is moribund – nothing works – the lift won't move – the hot water's cold – even the doorkey drops to pieces. Perhaps tomorrow morning it *will* be fine and I shall be able to linger and loiter all over the place – in this lovely rococo Square – under the triumphal arches, along the alleys in the Pépinière – sip vermouth on the cobble stones, and dream of Voltaire. I'm sure I hope so! – In the meantime I've written to A.M.[9] It was inevitable. Absurd to have come here without doing so, and yet, curiously enough, the two things are quite disconnected. Nobody I suppose, will believe this – R. least of all. As for A. himself – will he really suppose that I've come all this way for the sake of his beaux yeux? Probably he won't think much about it anyway; and then there's always a considerable chance that he won't be able to see me – that he'll be completely engrossed with women – has gone away – or heaven knows what – in which case the meeting won't come off, and things will be simplified. But it certainly is rather a singular coincidence. For years I've wanted to come and look at Nancy; at last, for a hundred and one odd reasons, I do so; and at that very moment A. is in Strasbourg. In my present mood, I must confess that, maddening as he is, I should like to see him. I should also like to see Strasbourg. Perhaps I'll get a letter on Thursday. We shall see. One of the most curious affairs of all is the affair of A.M.'s and this bids fair to be a characteristic chapter of it.

Alas! I've finished Lord Salisbury. (Vol. 3) The intelligent Lady Gwendolen lays everything out so clearly and admirably that it's sad to come to an end. And it's all so strange – though how strange the intelligent Lady Gwendolen doesn't quite realize. Another fact of the Victorian incomprehensibility. One gasps – glares – and passes on. Though, unlike Dante, one really can't help saying something.

Sept. 8th

> 'Mais, seigneur, s'il le faut, si le ciel en colère
> Réserve à d'autres yeux la gloire de vous plaire . . .'

Les yeux de Burton, for instance? But no! The anger of heaven has evolved a subtler form of vexation, since the days of Racine: – a mind that is pleased by almost every eye, and so in reality is never pleased at all. Célimène? Hardly – Manon? More nearly. But no matter – it is Racine that fills my thoughts here and now. This marvellous day! Exactly as I wished it! A

[9] Alistair MacDonald, nicknamed the Mooncalf.

day of floating, warmth, exploration vagueness. It is really charming of Nancy to have come out so magnificently well. The good King Stanislas be praised! And perhaps, also, Racine. For could the eighteenth century have existed without him? Everything in it seems always to be looking back to that triumphant miracle of form. Those exquisite palpitating Alexandrines are the bedrock of an age. The Place Stanislas is built on them. One steps under the triumphal arch, and down the Place de la Carrière, one turns to the right, to the left, is greeted by twin semi-circles of busts and pilasters, one comes upon the Porte Desilles, one paces back along the Cours Léopold – it is Racine all the way. But the father was greater than his children. They never quite recaptured that incredible combination of simplicity and subtlety – they ran to elegance, elaboration, pomp. Nobody can blame them – one can only be delighted – but the supreme curve was beyond them. That astonishing concatenation of gloire and plaire! It is so very nearly simply flat – and yet actually it sums up a whole dictionary of passion. I sat this morning in the lovely Pépinière, mouthing the lines – the parterres and the fountain in front of me, the comfortable trees above me, and . . . Rodin's odiously clever statue of Claude Lorrain well at my back. For a moment or two, on a seat in the sun, I was positively hot. I watched old ladies with their peeing dogs, children with paper windmills, the assignations of lovers. La gloire de vous plaire! It was time to go at last – to plunge under the Porte de la Craffe – on and on – till, just before lunch I found myself back again drinking vermouth in the Place Stanislas. Suddenly my notion of having a really cheap luncheon somewhere crumbled away, I thought I'd try the Café Stanislas, went in and found a gourmet's paradise. It looks as if all the rest of my time at Nancy will be dominated by an oscillation between the Café Stanislas and the Grand Hotel – across the Eastern corner of the Place – that's to say if my stomach will stand it. As for my purse, I cast all such considerations to the winds. But exercise will be essential if I'm to get through the succession of heavenly meals that I see stretching out in front of me, like the alternating cupids and bouquets on the cornice of the Hotel de Ville. To-day at any rate I did well, going, after my siesta, for an hour's walk to a distant church, built, like most of the rest of the town, by the admirable Héré, and containing the tomb of Stanislas himself.

So I was hungry enough for my dinner – during which rather a foolish incident took place. The table next me was reserved for one. Presently the guest arrived – one of those thin-lipped intellectual epicures, who correspond exactly to some of our friends who interest themselves in art. Enjoyment the one thing that is *not* present. With my neighbour, the severity and pedantry of taste was carried to its most ascetic pitch. He ate his melon like a scrupulous rabbit; and then, in flawless French, entered into elaborate and distressed dissertations with the waiters. 'Où est le maitre d'hotel?' etc. The French was in fact so flawless that I decided he must be an Englishman. The clothes seemed certainly English. No decoration in the button-hole. The only slightly suspicious object – and this really ought to have decided me – was a rather effeminate wrist watch. But I came to the conclusion that he must be some very distinguished member of the Civil Service – one of those infinitely cultivated and embittered eunuchs who, one must suppose, govern the country, and perhaps afford the most satisfactory explanation of its present plight. But really the wrist watch ought to have shown me that I was wrong. However, at last I determined, coûte qu'il coûte, to satisfy my curiosity. After a great deal of complicated manoeuvring of orders and counter-orders, he ate a fig. I also had figs; but before eating mine, I turned to him and said, in the most off-hand and idiomatic English style possible – 'Are these all right?' I calculated that if he'd been French he would have been quite at sea. As it was, there was a moment's hesitation, and he answered, with the precise politeness that one expected, 'They're excellent.' The question seemed solved, and I ate my fig, which, as a matter of fact, was not very good. But then doubt suddenly assailed me. Giving way to the instinct of the moment, I very rashly said – 'May I ask you another question? Are you an Englishman who speaks French very well, or a Frenchman who speaks English very well?' A faint – a very faint smile – appeared (for the first and last time) and he

174

answered 'I'm Italian.' This completely ruined me. The eventuality had never occurred to me; and I saw at once that he belonged to that dreariest of classes, the cosmopolitan, that he was doubtless merely a diplomat. At the same time – naturally, given his status – not the remotest sign of unbending: he coldly continued with his cigar. I had got into an impossible position – was being tacitly told I was a tiresome intruder – and all I could do was to depart in silence as soon as I could and with whatever dim dignity I could muster. A lesson, I suppose! But it was really all very amusing and well worth it.

Out in the Place again, I wandered incoherently for a little, then took a turn in the shadowy Pépinière-groves and grottoes stretching away into quite uncensored darkness – then back into the Place and into another and cheaper café, where the usual trio played selections from Gounod while I drank some cointreau. A couple of miserable lovers were having a desperate scene just opposite me. The man was near suicide, and the woman . . . far from it. I was reminded of that night at the Jardin des Gourmets when . . . ah no! no! Such things are not worth thinking about . . . I emerged again on to the Place, and drifted back to this hotel, and up to my bedroom, and on to my bed, where I am at the present moment. I've been writing for over an hour – it is half past eleven – all is quiet in Nancy . . . – La gloire de vous plaire! La gloire de vous plaire! –

Sept. 9th. Such a quiet, vague, dreamy day that there's nothing to say about it. A visit to the absurd local museum, an inspection of the strange chapel of the Dukes of Lorraine (which *still*, so the old lady in charge informed me, belongs to the House of Austria), and a little poking in second-hand bookshops – that's all. A perfect Frenchman – a Maugham without the twitch – gave an example at dinner at the Café Stanislas of how a meal *should* be ordered. Infinite quiet – and the maître d'hotel, almost immediately, seemed to spring out of the ground of his own accord – ah! the real thing!

Sept. 10th. Strasbourg – Hotel de la Maison Rouge – By no means expected! But a letter from A.M. made me decide this morning to come here at once. As he wants to come to Nancy on Saturday and is having examinations – poor creature! – here today and tomorrow, I realised that if I wanted to see Strasbourg this was my chance. With luck I shan't meet A.M. –it would only distract him if I did – and I seem to have chosen my time well, as the weather crumbled the moment I left Nancy, and it was raining here before night. A much better place to be in the rain than Nancy! In any case an extraordinary changement de décoration: straight from 18th century France to medieval Germany. I'd no idea how thoroughly teutonic this town was; everyone speaks German in the streets – everybody is German – the place is simply German – and how the French managed to get up such a hullabaloo about it I can't understand. The contrast in atmosphere is most marked. Good nature seems to surround one – even the waiters in the hotel restaurant tonight were charming – and the dashing little orchestra playing Weber in the café was another guess [sic] affair to the screeching trios of France. I rather wish I didn't have to go back tomorrow, but I foresee that if I stayed complications might arise. I should like to explore the curious streets, so full of disorder and vitality; and I should like to get more familiar with the really amazing Cathedral – the climax of Gothic, with its windows and its red stone which does look, as A. said in his letter, as if it would be nice to eat – an Edinburgh rock effect. And then, cheek by jowl with it, the 18th Century crops up again – the magnificent palace of the Cardinal de Rohan – all grey, calm, and stately, beside the flushed hysterical religiosity of the Middle Age. After walking round for about two hours, I was glad to get back to this hotel and have a bath before dinner. What a blessing to be able to afford such a thing! It means, as a rule, I find, paying 12 shillings a day for one's room, instead, I suppose, of 8, and it's certainly well worth it. But whether – vu the state of affairs in England and the world at large – such luxuries will be available very much longer remains to be seen. All the more reason to snatch them while one can – to plunge into a hot bath immediately, before the revolution comes and all the water's permanently cold!

If it's fine tomorrow, I mean to stop for an hour or two at Lunéville on the way back, and have a look at the scene of the drama of Mme du Châtelet's last days. After that it will be pleasant to be at the Grand Hotel again. The lift-boy – my only friend, apparently! – will welcome me. Aged 19, can talk a 'leetle' English, name so far unknown. The kind youth ran at top speed across the vast Place Stanislas and back this morning to get me a box of matches, just as I was starting off for the station. Dadie[10] would have done the same thing – also the Bronzino[11] – also A. (only he would have thrown the matchbox on the way back, on to the top of the statue of King Stanislas, and probably have been very nearly arrested) – Ralph would have produced a matchbox from his pocket – and R – of course it was quite obvious as soon as it started that this sentence was going to lead up to R – only this time my readers (if I ever have any) will be disappointed, because the sentence, after all, ends in . . . an aposiopesis!

A. typically enclosed in his letter a most disgusting little object – a minute ivory mascot of two dogs copulating – at least I suppose they were dogs and I suppose they were copulating – but the thing was so revolting that I hurriedly put it back into the envelope and nothing will induce me to look at it again. Perhaps really he won't turn up on Saturday – I shouldn't be at all surprised – and in some ways it would be a relief. I feel that he'll insist on my playing chess with him in a café and though his chess is amusing it is also exhausting – game after game after game. After all (I see myself reflecting) I didn't come to Nancy to play chess with a Mooncalf. But such is life – or rather, such is my life – a game of chess with a Mooncalf at Nancy – the height of the impossible and the bizarre.

I suppose he'll still be wearing the ring I gave him – the ring Henry[12] gave me. I admit I went rather far when I did that, but I really don't regret it. For one thing, the ring suits the creature, for another Henry, poor Henry – he had utterly disappeared

[10] George Rylands.
[11] Alan Searle. See p 164 n^3.
[12] Henry Lamb.

from my existence, and it means less than nothing to me now that he meant more than everything to me once. Oh God! Peppard! Hampstead! Donegal! The Lacket! Oh God, oh God! That I really should have gone through all that and come out of it not only alive but positively kicking! So altogether it's quite amusing to see A's finger decorated with Henry's ring.

I am happy – amused – energetic. It may all hang by a thread, I feel, but the thread holds. I must write to Mary [Hutchinson] and try to give her some notion of my condition – how admirably well she would appreciate it!

Sept. 11th. Back again at Nancy, but in the wretchedest weather. The rain and cold this morning were such that I gave up hope of seeing anything more of Strasbourg, and retired to my bedroom where I read the Abbé Duchesne's Histoire Ancienne de L'Eglise for an hour or so. A remarkable man, the Abbé – the description of him in Loisz's Memoirs is fascinating, and it was that that directed me to this book. A most classical writer; but the Voltarean tang which got the book, eventually, put on the Index, is so discreet that it's difficult to taste it. Otherwise a book that I've long wanted to have – 'Éloges de Madame Geoffrin', which I discovered in a second-hand bookshop here two days ago – has been entertaining me. It contains three descriptions of her (besides the well known passage in Marmontel) – the first by Morellet, the second by Thomas, the third by d'Alembert; and d'Alembert's is far the worst. – 'Comblé si long-temps de son amitié et de ses bontés, puis-je me refuser la triste consolation de verser aussi quelques et de tracer quelques mots sur cette tombe, déja couverte d'éloges et de larmes?' – An able mathematician, no doubt, and an admirable man, but *not* a good writer. The only thing that was new to me in the book came in a letter from Grimm to Mme G. in which he refers en passant to 'le ruisseau de la rue St Honoré': it calls up an excellent vision of the Paris of those days.

The screeching trio once more tonight. As I sat sipping my coffee, listening to the lamentable waltzes, and watching the young Italianate garçon, napkin in hand, explaining to his elder confrère, in interminable oratory, the disastrous progress

(I could only suppose) of his loves, my mind drifted in the dreamiest fashion. The initials I'd noticed just before on the towels in this hotel – the mystic initials 'G.H.' (they really simply signify 'Grand Hotel') set my speculations off in one direction. The muffled prelude! Will it ever be followed by anything at all approaching a fugue? A non-absorbing affair – idyllic – easy – would I fancy just suit me at the moment; but it's a mere toss up whether G.H. can supply it. Perhaps the G. is the most propitious thing about it. My thoughts floated from George to George. – G.B. – Dadie – George Mallory – George Lyttelton (a phantasm) – and at last George Underwood, the second of my desperate businesses at school. A very nice boy, I'm sure, rather fat and very freckled – destined to the army, into which he went; not long ago I saw his name in an Army List, and I suppose he's now a Senior Officer of nearly fifty with a wife and family – bald, with a few tufts of fading ginger hair – ah, his red hair that agitated me so romantically about thirty-five years ago! A short, podgy, good-natured figure, very popular in the mess . . . Now I think of it, there's a marked resemblance between my feelings for him and for R. I was older, and enormously devoted and obsessed; he was very sweet and very affectionate, but what he really liked was going off somewhere with Ruffus Clarke and the chic older boys, while I was left in the lurch, ruminating and desperate. How I loathed Ruffus Clarke! – a biggish, calm, very fair-haired boy – wicked and irresistible. I based my objections on purely moral grounds. I was a romantic prig, and the only wonder is how poor Underwood put up with me for a moment. And now, after thirty-five years . . . well, I hope I'm *slightly* more realistic. At any rate, I've had some fun in the interval.

Ruffus Clarke and Fell! I can see them with absolute distinctness. Both with that curious softness which some boys of about seventeen seem to be able to mingle with their brutality. Fell was handsome, dark and slightly sinister, though not nearly so sinister as his younger brother, who, sandy and hatchet-faced, had devilry written all over him. The elder Fell was kind – especially to me; my mental prestige impressed him. Ruffus Clarke didn't care about prestige or anything else. As for me, I never knew what really happened –

nobody told me – I couldn't even guess. I can guess now – but still not accurately; and I should still like to know all the details of those goings on – details, which, no doubt, not a creature living has the faintest memory of.

Lunéville was of course impossible. But I don't give up hope of seeing it – when I return, as I assuredly must, – to this pleasant country. The lift-boy's name is Emile.

Saturday, Sept. 12th. 5.30. As the approach of A. draws near – and he's due to arrive at 7 this evening – I begin to feel a little uneasy – partly because of this diary; I hardly see when I shall be able to write it, so long as he's buzzing about. Hence this unusual hour. Otherwise, experience warns me to expect no real satisfactions – except those of sentiment and oddity. Eternal chess, no doubt! – The sun, for a surprise, came out again this morning, and I strolled down to a triumphal arch I hadn't yet visited, past the barracks and the botanical gardens. The arch was charming, but the street it was in was smelly and decayed. France, with all her gold, seems pretty poverty- stricken. The beggars here are such as I've rarely seen – they look as if they'd all sat to their fellow townsman Callot – visions of utter horror and degradation. The soldiers are uncouth rustics with red noses and (about half of them) wear spectacles – which doesn't seem quite the thing. As for the botanical gardens, they are comic – a few hideous chrysanthemums and dahlias. I hurried back to the Place, where I found a chair in the sun outside the café of the trio, and ordered a glass of grenadine and seltzer. As I was sipping this degraded drink – my mind a blank – a motor, passing, slowed down – a female, slightly fashionable, looked in my direction and then seemed to murmur my name to her male companion. The motor stopped, and I automatically got up, thinking it might be Diana Cooper, but – such is my vagueness for faces –not at all sure. It was only when she introduced her companion a Mr Kommer (spelling doubtful)[13] that my hesitation disappeared. The truth was she was looking younger, more cheerful, and less like the Madonna than usual. They got out, and insisted on

[13] Spelling correct. Dr Rudolph Kommer, the enigmatic and remorselessly shaved 'dearest friend' of Lady Diana Cooper.

my motoring with them to the Café Stanislas – more expensive.
There we sat for some time. She was driving back from Venice –
with the ghastly-looking dago – an odd couple, but somehow or
other not in the least compromising. But why? Perhaps he was
paying. She mentioned my 'friends' in Venice –decidedly dimly, I
thought. She herself, she explained, after Duff's return home to
be made Under Secretary for War, had stayed with Mrs Corrigan
in a marvellous palazzo, etc. She was very agreeable; but I had, as
I always do for some mysterious reason with her, the sensation of
struggling vainly to show that I'm not a fool – mysterious,
because really her own comments are very far from being out of
the ordinary. K (or C) was polite. They admired Nancy; but it
was too early for lunch, and they had to hurry on to catch the
boat tomorrow at Calais. They went to their car, and then I
observed that there was another member of the party – a kind of
chauffeur, who sat in the dicky behind. He grinned a good deal –
rather tendenciously I thought; perhaps he was K (or C)'s man –
in every sense –, and I daresay the brightest of the three.

This highly unexpected meeting was less tiresome than
might have been supposed. The sun was still shining as they
drove off, and I wandered away in another direction, to find
some lunch in some new restaurant – placid and hungry.
Lunch over, I grubbed in a bookshop for a little, came back
here for my siesta, tottered out again to a teashop for tea,
paced about the town for an hour or so, buying picture
postcards, and so back once more here, to this diary. The non-
existence is amazing! But soon A.M. will be upon me. (Emile, I
forgot to say, ran out with his telegram to me, as I was strolling
in the Square). I'm a little afraid that his appearance may spoil
the unity of this tour. On the other hand, it may just add the
required accent to it. A little actuality . . . well! we shall see!

Sunday, Sept. 13th. He came last night. He went this evening –
to Paris; a shorter visit than I'd expected. Also, more successful
. . . What will happen to the poor child I can't imagine. Thank
goodness he's got the diploma he went to Strasbourg for two
months ago – a good deal to my surprise. He must have done a
little work and shown some capacity; but his future remains
extremely enigmatic – oscillating between an ushership at some

second-rate public school and an assistant consulship in some outlying colony. But his indolence is really pathological, and if it weren't for the fact that his family (apparently) has some money one would expect him to become what he himself at times half-suggests he may – a pimp or a tapette. The evening passed off well. We had an excellent dinner at the Stanislas – consommé, trout, partridge, an admirable Château Lafite – and then, at the trio café we drank coffee and played chess. Only two games, though, and they were amusing ones. He talked – enthusiastically and not unintelligently – about Madame Bovary, Beauty, affection, youth – they're moving qualities; and yet – I hardly know why – I wasn't moved very much. To get what one wants rather late in the day leaves one always, I suppose, with a feeling of flatness. But it would be absurd to complain, for everything that I wanted I had – without any fuss at all. Charming, really! Today we walked about, and he thoroughly appreciated the town, and at last there was some sun, so that, instead of going at 3 he stayed on till seven. He was full of Strasbourg – naturally. Hardly an enquiry about my doings – luckily: it would be quite a mistake for him to be interested in me. At moments, owing chiefly to his incredible slowness, my exasperation became intense – but he had no suspicion of it; and, when at last he had vanished, I did, for the first time since coming abroad, feel a little lonely. I missed him at dinner. But that soon passed off, and the pleasures of solitude are with me again. The freedom, and the sense (no doubt almost entirely illusory) of power!

All the same my mood (perhaps owing to a slight fatigue) has been on the whole elegiac this evening. Some feelings of remorse about R. – that I am being unkind – and the reflection that in this wretched world unkindness is out of place. Some doubts about what I really feel. Some regrets for what is unattainable – hardly imaginable, even – how feeble and ineffectual one is! In the café after dinner, listening to the trio, I dipped into a Napoleonic daydream – though it wasn't anything so crude as that. The young Italianate garçon, still explaining his disastrous armours, half-fascinated me. I went out at last into the cold dark Square, and walked up and down in a mingled state of depression and elevation. How difficult to say whether one is triumphant or baffled, happy or discontented, sublime or ridiculous, as one ranges through the past and the present, inspects the universe and oneself with an alarming detachment, and at the same time feels oneself agitated by passions which, even in such preposterous pages as these, one dares not describe!

Paris for me too tomorrow. I wish it were not so, and that I could find myself at Dover without the interlude of that altogether too engrossing place.

Sept. 14. Paris. Hotel Foyot. Yes, here I am back again – this time at Foyot's once more, as I felt I could hardly stand being on the other side of the river. It was sad leaving Nancy, which was at its brightest and best at midday when I departed. Farewell! Farewell! – To the spacious Place and all the gilding – to the arches - to the Pépinière. Farewell to the Grand – under whose roof, I discovered Marie Antoinette lodged on her way from Vienna to Paris to marry the Dauphin – Farewell to the Café Stanislas, and its low square room, so bright and so full of business-like hospitality, with Madame enthroned aloft, as severe and dominating as Ibsen. And farewell to the Café of the Trio, screeching still no doubt at this very moment, while the Italianate garçon expatiates forever upon his irremediably dilapidated loves. – It is cold here, though not altogether sunless. I've been all over the place buying tickets and trying feebly to rescue my lost shirts from the Berkeley. Dinner here – a good plain one. The waiters as ever. I suppose, by dint of keeping the windows tightly shut, I shall sleep in this noisy blue room. It seems rather absurd to be sitting at 10 o'clock, alone, with nothing but a solitary bed before me, in the middle of this frantic town. But I simply don't know where I could go or what I could do. I don't understand Montparnasse. I've no idea how or in what direction I could be improper. No! Solitude and sleep! That's all I'm fit for at the moment. Farewell, Nancy, farewell!

Sept. 15th. 10 a.m. It looks a nice day, and I am up, swathed in an overcoat, by the window, which gives a diagonal glimpse of the Luxembourg Gardens. What kind of life is this I lead? A singularly visionary one. The complete absence of letters or news from England has produced a strange vacuum in which I as often as not seem to myself to be a buzzing chimera. But it has really been a very pleasant relaxation. Already it's slipping into the past. Tomorrow presumably I shall find letters in Gordon Square, and real life will begin again. Among them, will there be one from R? Heaven knows. As I re-approach him, it's difficult at moments not to feel uneasy again. Actually, I don't even know where he is – he may still be in France, drinking cocktails with Burton. Or he may be back in London, drinking cocktails with Jock Hunter. It's futile to speculate – or indeed to think of the future in that direction at all. But 24 hours ago I didn't have to remind myself of that – I felt no instinct to speculate – my mind wandered in a happy freedom . . . and now the tiresome compulsion re-appears. Away with it! Today at any rate shall be devoted to absolute drifting – looking at old books and pictures – errand boys and aged whores – gardens and street-corners. My great object will be to avoid the Colonial Exhibition. Some portraits of Degas attract me – and then my capacity for idling is almost equal to the Mooncalf's. I shall all too easily get through the day.

Midnight. So I went into the garden – the lovely Luxembourg, which was all that one could wish in the brilliant morning light. The height of Frenchness – crowded, happy, ordered. The trees were beginning to turn, and I thought of that time – almost exactly twenty years ago – September, but I think the very end of September, 1911 – when I walked there after my visit to Henry in Brittany, after a night journey through Nantes. Where I stayed in Paris I haven't any idea, but my remembrance of the gardens is vivid, and my sudden excitement in them. After the discomfort, illness, and emotional failure of the Brittany week, an extraordinary sense of vitality and excitement came upon me; a spring of self-confidence gushed up; I felt able and ready to face the world – it was delightful and astonishing. That summer I had finished my book on French Literature, but it was not yet published. I was 31, and life was still before me . . . This morning I was happy too, but less excitedly; and I thought also of that other curious visit, not so very long ago, with C, in the intense heat, when I crept out, half dead with exhaustion, to try and get a little air under the trees. But I didn't succeed, and had to creep back to bed in this hotel, where I remained till Ralph came and rescued

us . . . Leaving the gardens, I walked up the Rue de Seine, and
into a bookshop where I collapsed before some marvellous
Corneilles, coming out after quite a long time having spent about
£5. Then into the Boulevard St-Germain to the Café of the Deux
Magots, where I sat drinking vermouth in the sun and gazing at
the charming little church of St Germain des Prés. As I did so, a
figure came across the street towards me – familiar – in a moment
I saw it was John Banting. He was gay, amusing, and I was very
glad to see him, and, apparently he me. He cut an engagement for
lunch for me, told me of his latest affair, chattered away about art
and adventures, till we got into a taxi to drive to a restaurant he
knew of. As we started off, we both saw, sitting on the other side
of the café, Peter Morris, alone, reading. We stopped the taxi, to
ask him to join us, but he had had lunch already, so we went on
without him, promising to return for coffee. Lunch outside a tiny
place in the Cité. Then back to the Magots and Peter. It was none
of it at all what I expected when I'd set out – I'd been quite
convinced that I should meet nobody I knew; and there I was,
talking with these two creatures, as if we were at the Ivy. At last I
left them, coming back here for a brief siesta, after which I
whisked off to the Musée de L'Orangerie in the Tuileries to see
the exhibition of portraits by Degas. The pictures were fascinating – so exquisite, witty, and serious – and there were admirable
sculptured studies too, in bronze. Then a stroll down the
Tuileries Gardens – how supremely enjoyable it all was! My old
dread and dislike of Paris melted into nothing in the shining sun.
A rainbow in the fountain – the long alley beyond – the
magnificent Louvre closing in the distance – nothing but radiance
and exhilaration. A little tea in the Rue de Rivoli – a taxi back
here. Rest and a bath. Arrival of Peter Morris – the darling! – for
dinner. We went off to the Escargot, where we had a delicious
meal. Back again here, to this room, where we've been talking
until now. He has gone and I am left alone, rather breathless,
after such a glorious day. The megrims of the morning quite
vanished! Let those problems (which I've now almost forgotten) solve themselves! Peter was amusing about his visit to
Rome at Easter, and the emotional complications (which I'd
had no idea of) between him, Duncan, and Jemmy. His
singular and ill-fated escapade with a waiter at Sorrento – etc.

etc. He was looking very well – but professed himself gloomy – about his feeble character, his non-accomplishment of what his ambitions indicate, his increasing age. I tried to reassure him – and surely nothing can be very wrong with such a rare and exquisite being as he. We were affectionate – voilà tout. His hair had regained all its old enchantment – it was the last thing I saw as he vanished down the hotel stairs.

Wed. Sept. 16th. 10 a.m. Really the weather might have thought of something a little more original than this. Such a feeble old joke, to sulk until the last minute and then come out in a blaze when it's too late! What with this beauty and Peter combined I might perhaps have stayed on here – if I hadn't taken my place in the train and sent telegrams announcing my arrival. It seems rather mad to go – and yet I daresay in reality most of the effect depends upon its transitoriness; besides I'm beginning to want to be in England again. I think perhaps Ralph may be back by this time, which would be delightful; and then – C! – and all the pleasures of Ham Spray!

Peter's existence here is certainly singular. He's taken a room in a shabby little hotel in the Rue des Saints Pères. He does, apparently, nothing – drifts – reads Evelina (so charming of him to read Evelina) at the Deux Magots. He hasn't got an overcoat. Of his three shirts, two are now too dirty to wear, and the third will very shortly become so; and what will happen then? He is incapable – and he adduces this as the final proof of his spiritual degeneracy – radically incapable of sending anything to the wash. He looks at people whom he thinks attractive, and imagines having a dim affair with them. And so the days pass. Rather a waste, one cannot help thinking – a gem of purest ray serene, etc. It's possible, though, that, in reality, he's waiting – for some signal from England.

Well, I must pack, and tell them to get my bill ready. I wish I was like K. (or C.) and had a man! But even that would impinge upon my freedom – which has been so absolute. And now it's dwindling, dwindling. The flêche d'or awaits me. I must get in and roll off – to what? – London, Ham Spray, the London Library, the Oriental, notions of work, notions of love, R., and, in short, ordinary life!